HOW TO WRITE SCIENCE FICTION AND FANTASY

ORSON SCOTT CARD

Writer's Digest Books

Cincinnati, Ohio

Contents

To my sister Janice,
Who taught me how to read,
Which was the beginning of wisdom,
And how to be charitable,
Which is wisdom's end.

About the Author

*N*o one had ever won both the Hugo and the Nebula Award for best science fiction novel two years in a row—until 1987, when *Speaker for the Dead* won the same awards given to *Ender's Game*. But Orson Scott Card's experience is not limited to one genre or form of storytelling. A dozen of his plays have been produced in regional theatre; his historical novel, *Saints* (alias *Women of Destiny*) has been an underground hit for several years; and Card has written hundreds of audio plays and a dozen scripts for animated videoplays for the family market. He has also edited books, magazines, and anthologies; he writes a regular review column for *The Magazine of Fantasy and Science Fiction*; he publishes *Short Form*, a journal of short-fiction criticism; he even reviews computer games for *Compute!* Along the way, Card earned a master's degree in literature and has an abiding love for Chaucer, Shakespeare, Boccaccio, and the Medieval Romance. He has taught writing courses at several universities and at such workshops as Antioch, Clarion, Clarion West, and the Cape Cod Writers Workshop. It is fair to say that Orson Scott Card has examined storytelling from every angle.

Born in Richland, Washington, Card grew up in California, Arizona, and Utah. He lived in Brazil for two years as an unpaid missionary for the Mormon Church and received degrees from Brigham Young University and the University of Utah. He currently lives in Greensboro, North Carolina, with his wife, Kristine, and their three children, Geoffrey, Emily, and Charles (named for Chaucer, Brontë, and Dickens).

Introduction

A writer never knows who's going to be reading his book, but I've made a few assumptions about you, anyway. I figure that you're probably not yet an established writer in the genre of speculative fiction, or you wouldn't feel a need to read a book on how to write it. Still, you have a genuine interest in writing science fiction and fantasy, not because you have some notion that it's somehow "easier" to make a buck in this field (if that's your delusion, give it up at once!), but rather because you believe that the kind of story you want to tell might be best received by the science fiction and fantasy audience.

I hope you're right, because in many ways this is the best audience in the world to write for. They're open-minded and intelligent. They want to think as well as feel, understand as well as dream. Above all, they want to be led into places that no one has ever visited before. It's a privilege to tell stories to these readers, and an honor when they applaud the tales you tell.

What I can't do in a book this brief is tell you everything you need to know about writing fiction. What I *can* do is tell you everything I know about how to write speculative fiction *in particular*. I've written a whole book on characterization and point of view, so I hardly need to cover that same material here; nor will I attempt to teach you plotting or style, dialogue or marketing or copyright law or any of the other things that writers of *every* kind of fiction have to know something about. But I can attempt to tell you the things that *only* the writers of speculative fiction need to worry about: world creation, alien societies, the rules of magic, rigorous extrapolation of possible futures — tasks that don't come up in your average mystery or romance or literary tale.

To do that, I've divided this book into five chapters of varying length. Chapter I deals with the boundaries of speculative fiction; it's an essay on what science fiction and fantasy are, so that you can get an idea of the range of possibilities and educate yourself with the literature that has gone before.

Chapter II, the longest, begins the practical, hands-on work of world creation, perhaps the most vital step in creating a good speculative story.

Chapter III deals with the structuring of a science fiction or fantasy tale—how you go about turning your world into a story, or making your story work well within its world.

With Chapter IV, we go through the actual writing process, dealing with the problems of exposition and language that only speculative fiction writers face.

The first part of Chapter V deals with the practical business of selling science fiction and fantasy—though you'd better check the copyright date on this edition of the book before acting on my advice, since this is the section most likely to become outdated.

And also in Chapter V we get a little personal and I offer you some advice on how to live successfully as a science fiction or fantasy writer. Not that I know how you should live your life—but I have made some really first-rate mistakes in my time, and have seen others make some doozies, too, and if by forewarning you I can forearm you, I think it's worth the effort.

1. The Infinite Boundary

*I*t was 1975. I was twenty-four years old. The naive ambitions of youth were beginning to be tempered by reality.

I had written a couple of dozen plays and more than half of them had been produced in college or community theatres—for a total remuneration of about $300. At that rate, I figured, I had only to write sixteen full-length plays a week to make $10,000 a year—hardly major money, even then. And I was fast, but not *that* fast.

Furthermore, the non-profit theatre company I had started was tumbling toward bankruptcy with all its debts looming over me. My day job as an editor with a university press didn't pay me enough to live on, let alone pay what the company owed. The only thing I knew how to do that had any hope of bringing in extra money was writing—and it was plain that I'd have to find something to write besides plays.

I had dabbled in science fiction for years, reading quite a bit of it, even trying my hand at a few stories. For a while in my late teens I had even worked on a cycle of stories tracing the development of a family with peculiar psychic abilities as they worked out their genetic destiny on a colony planet. Now, with new enthusiasm—or was it desperation?—I dusted off the best of them, one that had once earned a nice note from an editor, and proceeded to rewrite it from beginning to end.

It was the tale of a wandering tinker who had a psionic gift that manifested itself in two ways: He could communicate with birds, and he could heal the sick. When he returned to his hometown, Worthing, a medievalish village deep in the Forest of Waters, he came into conflict with the villagers over their treatment of his birds; eventually he was blamed for an epidemic that carried off many villagers during a devastating winter storm, and they killed him.

3

In short, it was the sort of *perky, cheerful little* tale that I've been writing ever since.

As I rewrote "Tinker," I was delighted to see how terrible the earlier version had been. After all, if I could see, at twenty-four, how bad the story was that looked so brilliant to me at nineteen, it must mean I had learned something in the intervening years. So it was with high hopes that I typed the new draft, tucked it into an envelope and mailed it away to *Analog* magazine.

Why *Analog*? Because in those days it was the only science fiction magazine that was listed in *Writer's Market*. I had never actually read an issue of the magazine. Still, my story was science fiction, and *Analog* was a science fiction magazine. What could be more logical?

The story came back in due course, rejected. But there was something in the accompanying letter to encourage me. Ben Bova, then editor of *Analog*, told me that he liked the way I wrote and hoped to see more stories from me.

So why was he rejecting "Tinker"?

Because it wasn't science fiction. "*Analog* publishes only science fiction," said Ben, so of course a fantasy like "Tinker" simply wouldn't do.

I was outraged—at first. "Tinker" had psionic powers, a colony planet, a far future time period—if that wasn't science fiction, what was?

Until I looked again at the story the way Ben Bova must have seen it. He knew nothing about the other stories in the cycle. "Tinker" included no mention of its taking place on a world being colonized by human beings, and there was nothing alien about the landscape. It could have been an English village in about 950 A.D.

As for John Tinker's psionic powers, there was nothing in the story to suggest they weren't *magical* powers. There was nothing to suggest they *were*, either, of course—he chanted no spells, rubbed no talisman, prayed to no pagan deity.

But in the absence of other evidence, the landscape clearly marked "Tinker" as fantasy. It was all those trees in the Forest of Waters. A rustic setting always suggests fantasy; to suggest science fiction, you need sheet metal and plastic. You need *rivets*. The buildings in "Tinker" didn't even use *nails*!

I had discovered the first kind of boundary that marks the twin genres of fantasy and science fiction: the publishing category.

Boundary 1: A Publishing Category

When fiction publishers send out books through the distributors and on to the bookstores, they have few ways of influencing the way those books are displayed and handled. Naturally, every publisher would like to see all his novels displayed face out on the shelves, preferably in a section labeled "New and Brilliant." But in the real world, this is not going to happen. Instead, most novels will be crammed spine out into the store's precious shelf space, with only the alphabetical accident of the author's last name deciding where on the shelf the books will be placed.

Having to browse through a thousand spine-out volumes grouped by the last names of authors he's never heard of would be quite inconvenient for the novel-buyer, of course. Fortunately, fiction publishers learned something from the nonfiction side of the business, which groups books by super-subjects, or categories. *How to Cross-Stitch* is grouped with *Plumbing Made Easy* under "How-to Books." Biographies are grouped by the last name of the *subject* rather than the *author*; history is roughly grouped by region and time period. New categories spring up as needed — in 1975, there was no bookstore section labeled "Computers."

Why not group fiction in a similar way? Micro-subjects wouldn't do — it wouldn't be practical to have sections called "Dog Stories," "Horse Stories," "Mid-life Crisis and Adultery," "Writers and Artists Struggling to Discover Themselves," "People in Past Eras Who Think and Talk Just Like Modern Americans," and "Reminiscences of Childhoods in Which Nothing Happened," even though these are all fairly popular themes for fiction.

But there *were* some broad categories that were quite useful, like "Science Fiction," "Fantasy," "Historicals," "Romances," "Mysteries," and "Westerns." Anything that didn't fit into the categories was lumped together under the heading "Fiction." Publishers could slap these labels on their books and know that bookstore owners — who couldn't possibly be familiar with, let alone read, every work by every author — would know how to group these books within the store so that readers could find them more easily.

For many years, the appetite of science fiction readers far outstripped the production of science fiction writers and publishers. About 30,000 or 40,000 readers were so hungry for another sf novel that they'd buy *anything*, however bad it might be, as long as it had a rocket on the cover. As

5

a result, while science fiction never sold very much, it *did* sell a certain guaranteed minimum. You couldn't lose money publishing it, almost regardless of quality.

As a result, the publishing category was able to nurture many young, talented, but utterly inept writers as they served their apprenticeships and eventually learned how to write. Unlike the literary genre, where first novels often sell in the hundreds rather than the thousands, promising but clumsy sf writers could live on the advances and royalties from sales of 40,000 books. And a surprising number of us whose inept first novels exposed more of our weaknesses than our strengths eventually learned how to turn in work that had polish—and, sometimes, depth.

Those days have passed, however. The ceiling has come off the genre, with hardcovers by Herbert, McCaffrey, Asimov, Heinlein, Clarke, and Douglas Adams all having hit the best-seller lists in the 1970s and 1980s. But the floor has also dropped out of the genre. As soon as there were big bucks to be made in science fiction and fantasy, publishers began to bring out more and more novels, until it was impossible for anyone to read half of them, let alone all. Instead of 40,000 readers buying one copy of everything, there were hundreds of thousands of readers buying copies of maybe half the books, and some books that almost nobody read.

The fantasy genre followed the same track with book publishing—only it was compressed into a much shorter time. With the word-of-mouth success of Tolkien's *Lord of the Rings* trilogy and *The Hobbit*, the fantasy genre was born in the late sixties. Only a few years later, Ballantine published Terry Brooks's *Sword of Shannara* and hit the best-seller lists. At once fantasy was as big a business as science fiction was becoming.

The appetite for new writers in the field of speculative fiction (science fiction and fantasy) is still enormous. If you write competently and if your story has any spark of life, you will sell it. And, while you no longer have the guarantee that even your weakest early work will be read and remembered, that can also be a blessing: I'm certainly glad that my first novel isn't trotted out and displayed wherever I go.

New writers are, if anything, even *more* welcome in the magazines. Here, too, the publishing categories matter. While the two most prestigious magazines, *Isaac Asimov's Science Fiction Magazine* (hereafter called *Asimov's*) and *The Magazine of Fantasy and Science Fiction* (*F&SF*), will occasionally publish rustic fantasies, all the magazines *prefer* science fiction with rivets and plastic. And not because that is necessarily the editors' taste, but because that's what the majority of the magazine-buying audience wants most and rewards best, with sales, with favorable letters of comment, and with Nebula and Hugo awards. The other two major magazines, *Omni* (which pays billions of dollars but buys only two stories an issue) and *Analog*, won't even consider rustic fantasy, though *Omni* will occasionally buy a contemporary or urban fantasy—the kind of story where something magical is happening in a familiar high-tech environment.

All these magazines pride themselves on publishing stories from new writers. What doesn't get told quite as often is that they *survive* by discovering new writers. There's a cycle in science fiction that most writers follow. They break into the field by selling short stories and novelettes to the magazines until their names and styles become familiar to book editors. Then they sign a few book contracts, get some novels under their belts, and suddenly they don't have time for those $400 stories anymore. The magazines that nurtured them and gave them their starts watch as the novels flow and the short fiction trickles in. So the magazines are forced to search constantly for new talent.

This is even more true with the newer and smaller markets. *Aboriginal SF* and *Amazing Stories*—the newest and oldest magazines in the field—have much smaller impact on the field, in part because the strongest writers are generally selling to *Omni*, *Asimov's*, and *F&SF*. But because of that, *Abo* and *Amazing* are that much more open to newcomers.

In practical terms, you'll have a better chance selling to the magazines if your story is (1) short and (2) science fiction rather than fantasy. My career followed that track; so did the careers of most other science fiction writers in the field. Only fantasy writers are virtually forced to begin selling at novel length because the market is so much smaller for fantasy.

Boundary 2: A Community of Readers and Writers

It's important to remember that there was a time when every one of today's publishing categories was part of the mainstream of fiction. When *Gone with the Wind* was published it was simply a novel, not a "historical" or a "romance"—though it would almost certainly be categorized that way today. And back when H. G. Wells, Jules Verne, A. Merritt, H. Rider Haggard, and others were inventing the genre of science fiction, their novels were published and displayed right alongside contemporaries like James, Dreiser, Woolf, and Conrad.

Yet there was a clear difference even in the early 1900s between incipient science fiction, fantasy, and all the rest of literature. It was hard to put it into words then. H. G. Wells's *The Time Machine, The War of the Worlds*, and *The Invisible Man* were wildly different from each other, yet alike in the sense that they dealt with advances in science; hence he called these novels "scientific romances."

This surely made them similar to the works of Jules Verne, who also dealt with scientific advances in novels like *Twenty Thousand Leagues Under the Sea*. But Verne never seemed to see danger or a dark side in advancing technology, and in the long run his novels were never so much about the science as about the sights and wonders to be found in strange, inaccessible places. *Twenty Thousand Leagues* wasn't *about* Nemo's submarine as much as it was about the marvelous sights to be seen from its portholes. *Journey to the Center of the Earth* was about survival in a strange, hostile environment, and included such delightful nonsense as the ruins of ancient Atlantis and dinosaurs that had survived deep in the bowels of the Earth.

Wells was much more serious and logical than Verne in his extrapolation of the possible results of scientific advances. And yet their stories sometimes had quite similar structures. For instance, while *Around the World in Eighty Days* dealt entirely with the sights and wonders of Verne's contemporary world, its ending absolutely hinges on knowledge of a scientific fact—that by traveling toward the east, the hero gained a day when he crossed the International Date Line. This is very much the same sort of structural game Wells played when he had the invaders from Mars in *The War of the Worlds* defeated by the common cold. Great events are changed by the most humble of facts—and yet when the reader reaches the surprise resolution, his faith in the order of the universe is restored. Humble little facts will save us in the end.

A. Merritt's *Face in the Abyss* and H. Rider Haggard's *She* had even less in common with Wells than Verne did. Both these novels have a traveler find himself in a land long forgotten by modern man. In *She*, a magnificent woman has found a way to live forever, at the cost of the blood of her subjects; in *The Face in the Abyss*, lizard men descended from the dinosaurs keep a race of humans in thrall for their obscene sports and pleasures. There is more of magic than science in both of these books, yet there was a strong overlap of the readers who loved Wells, those who loved Verne, and those who loved Merritt and Haggard.

Indeed, when Hugo Gernsback founded the first magazine devoted entirely to science fiction, *Amazing Stories*, back in the late twenties, he announced that he wanted to publish scientific romances like those of H.G. Wells; yet it is fair to say that, instead of the serious, rigorous scientific extrapolation found in Wells's work, Gernsback's magazine — and the others that soon imitated it — published stories that had far more of Verne's love of machines or of Merritt's and Haggard's romps into strange and dangerous places than of Wells's more serious treatment of science and the future. It wasn't until the mid-thirties, when John W. Campbell became editor of *Astounding* (now *Analog*), that Wellsian science fiction came to the fore in the American magazines.

Rigorous extrapolation, a gosh-wow love of gadgets, and mystical adventures in strange and mysterious places; every major stream in speculative fiction today can be traced back to authors who were writing before the publishing categories existed. From among the readers in the twenties and thirties who loved any or all of these authors arose the first generation of "science fiction writers," who knew themselves to be continuing in a trail that had been blazed by giants. Gernsback's publishing category of science fiction was a recognition of a community that already existed; once it was named, once it became self-conscious, that community blossomed and cast many seeds, giving rise to each new generation that repeats, revises, or reinvents the same literary tradition.

The boundaries that once were fluid now are much more firm, because the publishing category reinforces the identity of the community of readers and writers. Hilton felt no qualms about writing a lost-land novel, *Lost Horizon*; it troubled no one that it didn't belong in the same category as, say, his novel *Good-bye, Mr. Chips*. And so many readers responded to the book that the name of the lost land, Shangri-la, passed into the common language.

Today, though, an author who wrote a fantasy like *Lost Horizon* would immediately be placed into the fantasy category, and if he then wrote a *Good-bye, Mr. Chips*, American publishers would be at a loss as to where to place it. How could you call it fantasy? Yet if you publish it out of the fantasy category, the readers who liked the author's earlier books won't ever find it, and the readers who *do* browse the "Fiction" category won't ever have heard of this author and will probably pass the novel by. As a result there will be enormous pressure on the author to write "more books like that Shangri-la book."

(Indeed, he will be pressed to write a whole series, which will be promoted as "The Shangri-la Trilogy" until a fourth book is published, then as "The Shangri-la Saga" until the author is dead. It happened to Frank Herbert with his Dune books, and despite her best efforts it is happening to Anne McCaffrey with her dragon books. Only a few, like Marion Zimmer Bradley, manage to break out of such channels and take a sizeable audience with them.)

Yet my experience as a reader is that the category boundaries mean very little. There have been months, even years of my life when all I really wanted to read was science fiction; but I felt no shame or guilt, no enormous mental stretch when at other times I read historicals or mysteries, classics, poetry, or contemporary best sellers. At present my pleasure reading is history and biography, but that will certainly change again. And even at the height of a science fiction reading binge, nothing can stop me from devouring the latest John Hersey or William Goldman or Robert Parker novel.

The result is that today, while readers are very free, passing easily from one community to another, the publishing categories clamp down like a vise on the authors themselves. You must keep this in mind as you begin to publish. Do you wish to be forever known as a science fiction or fantasy writer?

Some writers whose careers have been largely based on science fiction writing have never been categorized that way. Kurt Vonnegut, for instance, stoutly resisted any claim that what he wrote was science fiction — though there is no definition of science fiction that does not include his novels within the genre *except* that the words science fiction have never been printed on his books.

John Hersey, as another example, has written such science fiction masterpieces as *White Lotus*, *The Child Buyer*, and *My Petition for More Space*; yet because he wrote other kinds of fiction first, he has never been locked into one category. ("Couldn't you, like, put some aliens into this book, Mr. Hersey? I'm not sure your audience will know what to make of this historical set in China of all places.")

Vonnegut and Hersey were never within the science fiction ghetto. A few rare writers like Bradbury and LeGuin have transcended the boundaries without compromising the elements of fantasy within their work.

But most of us find that the better we do as speculative fiction writers, the *less* interested publishers are in our non-sf, non-fantasy writing.

Boundary 3: What SF Writers Write Is SF

One surprising result of the ghettoizing of speculative fiction, however, is that writers have enormous freedom within its walls. It's as if, having once confined us within our cage, the keepers of the zoo of literature don't much care what we do as long as we stay behind bars.

What we've done is make the categories of science fiction and fantasy larger, freer, and more inclusive than any other genre of contemporary literature. We have room for everybody, and we are extraordinarily open to genuine experimentation.

Admittedly, *Isaac Asimov's Science Fiction Magazine* regularly receives letters that ask, "In what sense is this story by Kim Stanley Robinson or Karen Joy Fowler a science fiction or fantasy story? Why isn't it appearing in *Atlantic* where it belongs?" Some readers complain; indeed, some fairly howl at what writers do under the rubric of sf and fantasy.

Yet the reason these stories don't appear in *Atlantic* or *Harper's* or *The New Yorker* is that even though they aren't really science fiction or fantasy in the publishing-category sense or the community sense (there are neither rivets nor trees, neither science nor magic, and they certainly aren't what readers were consciously looking for) their stories are nevertheless strange, in ways that editors outside the field of sf and fantasy find quite threatening.

There is no particular reason why Karen Joy Fowler's "Tonto at 40" (published as "The Faithful Companion at 40" to avoid a lawsuit from the *Lone Ranger* people, who have no sense of fun) shouldn't have appeared in a literary magazine. But the story was too experimental, too odd in ways that felt dangerous or confusing to editors who are used to seeing only the "experiments" that follow the latest trend. Only within speculative fiction was there room for Fowler's work.

It has happened again and again, until it seems that there must be more room inside the ghetto walls than outside them. Even writers like Bruce Sterling and Lew Shiner, who have complained about the boneheadedness and unoriginality of most speculative fiction, discover that, despite the science fiction community's enormous appetite for stories with very bad thinking and worse writing, it remains the community most willing to sample something new.

Sample — not necessarily embrace. It is not experimental but traditional work that wins Hugo and Nebula awards within the field. What matters is that truly unfamiliar and untraditional work is published *at all*, first in the magazines, and, once the work has become somewhat familiar there, eventually in books.

In the long run, then, whatever is published within the field of science fiction and fantasy *is* science fiction and fantasy, and if it doesn't resemble what science fiction and fantasy were twenty years ago or even five years ago, some readers and writers will howl, but others will hear the new voice and see the new vision with delight.

Once, frustrated with the plethora of meaningless definitions of science fiction, Damon Knight said, "Science fiction is what I point at when I say science fiction." That may sound like a decision not to define the field at all — but it is, in fact, the only completely accurate definition.

The operative word in Damon Knight's definition is *I*. That is, if Damon Knight, a writer, critic, and editor of known credentials, says that a work is science fiction, then it is. When it comes to known science fiction writers, that power is almost absolute. Because I've been around long enough, if I write a book and decide to call it fantasy or science fiction, then it *is*; even if others argue with me, it will still be counted as part of my science fiction/fantasy oeuvre. If you doubt me, read Gene Wolfe's novel *Free Live Free*. He swears it's science fiction. There are even shreds of evidence within the novel that it might be so. That's enough for him, and so it is enough for us.

Editors and critics have the power to dub other people's work as well. If the editor at *Asimov's*, *Fantasy and Science Fiction*, *Analog*, *Aboriginal SF*, or *Omni* buys and publishes a story as fantasy or science fiction, then that writer's identity as an author of fantasy or science fiction is fairly launched.

Book publishers have similar authority. Patricia Geary was more than a little surprised to wake up one day and discover that her novels, including the brilliant *Strange Toys*, had been published by Bantam in the science fiction/fantasy category. The thought that she was writing within a "category" never entered her mind. But she quickly learned that whether she sought the label or not, the speculative fiction audience was open to her stories in a way that her intended "literary" audience was not.

Like the stable in C. S. Lewis's last Narnia book, *The Last Battle*, the science fiction ghetto is much larger on the inside than it is on the outside. You think as you enter it that you'll be cramped and confined; but I can tell you that for many of you it is only inside the sf community that you will find room enough to write all that you want to write and still find an audience for it.

Still, all this talk of freedom is pretty irrelevant to you. Why? Because unless you are already established as a science fiction or fantasy writer, you do *not* have the power to decide unilaterally that your work belongs in the category. You must persuade at least one editor that your novel or story is science fiction or fantasy — and with rare exceptions, editors have a finely discriminating eye.

You see, while the marketing department at a publishing house may think that a spaceship on the cover is enough to make a book sci-fi, the editorial department knows better. Your story has to *feel* like science fiction or fantasy to the editor or it won't get published, and then you won't have access to the great freedom that speculative fiction writers get *after* they've become established in the field.

So you need some sort of definition of speculative fiction that lets you know how to satisfy enough of the expectations of the genre so that editors will agree that your work belongs in the category. Let's take for granted at this point that your skills and innate genius make your stories publishable. You still need to make sure your story warrants being published *as science fiction or fantasy*.

The most complete definition will come to you only one way, and it isn't easy. You have to know everything ever published as speculative fiction or fantasy. Of course, you want to begin writing sf and fantasy *before* you die, so you know that you can't read every single book or story. You'll have to read a representative sample to get a feel for what has already been done in the field.

What makes this complicated is that the genres of science fiction and fantasy include not only what speculative fiction writers are writing now, but also everything they have ever written. This is because the entire history of speculative fiction as a self-conscious genre spans a single lifetime. Jack Williamson, for instance, was writing in the 1930s, when the adventure tradition of Merritt and Haggard and the gosh-wow science of Verne predominated. He is still writing today, producing work that is taken seriously by the most modern and sophisticated of speculative fiction readers.

Fiction from every period of speculative fiction is still in print, not because it is required reading in college and high school English classes — thankfully it isn't — but because the community of speculative fiction readers keeps it alive.

Go into the sf/fantasy section of your bookstore and you'll find both recent works and early, seminal books by living authors like Aldiss, Asimov, Bradbury, Clarke, Ellison, LeGuin, and Norton.

In the same section you'll find books by late great writers like Alfred Bester, James Blish, Edgar Rice Burroughs, Robert Heinlein, Robert Howard, E. E. "Doc" Smith, and J. R. R. Tolkien.

You'll also find relatively young writers like Larry Niven, Anne McCaffrey, Jack Chalker, C. J. Cherryh, David Drake, Octavia Butler, and Roger Zelazny.

And there'll be books by writers so new they have only a handful of titles in print, like Charles de Lint, William Gibson, Lisa Goldstein, James Patrick Kelly, Megan Lindholm, Pat Murphy, Pamela Sargent, and Bruce Sterling.

In fact, that's not a bad reading list, though it's far from complete. Even if you've already read quite a bit of science fiction, if any of those names sound unfamiliar to you then you need to do some homework. Pick several names from each group, buy a couple of inexpensive paperbacks by each author you choose, and read. You'll begin to get a sense of the breadth and depth of this field you're planning to write in. Some of the books you won't care for a bit. Some you'll admire. Some you'll love. Some will transform you.

Still, all that reading can take months. Though you'll have to do it eventually, you can start your education as a science fiction reader more modestly. Get a good overview of the field — I suggest David Hartwell's book *Age of Wonder: Exploring the World of Science Fiction* or James Gunn's *Alternate Worlds: The Illustrated History of Science Fiction*. Then get your hands on these great anthologies: *The Science Fiction Hall of Fame* (ed. Silverberg, Bova), *Dangerous Visions* and *Again, Dangerous Visions* (ed. Ellison), and *The Best of the Nebulas* (ed. Bova). Finally, subscribe to *Asimov's* and *F&SF* and read them from cover to cover every month; you should also sample *Analog*, *Aboriginal SF*, *Omni*, and *Amazing Stories*.

The Science Fiction Hall of Fame is an anthology of the short stories, novelettes, and novellas voted by the Science Fiction Writers of America as the best ever published up to 1966, the year that the SFWA was organized. There is no better collection of classic short science fiction from the 1930s, 1940s, and 1950s.

Dangerous Visions and its sequel, *Again, Dangerous Visions*, were meant by editor Harlan Ellison to be anthologies of work considered too dangerous to appear in the magazines. However, before *Again, Dangerous Visions* came out, the magazines themselves had been transformed enough that the stories didn't seem so dangerous anymore. It doesn't matter — they are an excellent snapshot of most of the best writers producing innovative short fiction during the sixties and early seventies, most of whom are still major figures in the field today.

The Best of the Nebulas is an anthology of the Nebula-winning short stories, novelettes, and novellas published between 1966 and 1986 that were voted best by the members of the SFWA in the late 1980s.

And the current issues of the magazines will show you what is happening right this minute in the field of speculative fiction.

Read all this and you'll have a very good sense, not only of what science fiction (and to a lesser degree fantasy) has been and is becoming, but also of what sort of science fiction you are drawn to.

You may discover that your taste in science fiction is quite old-fashioned — that you don't like most of the stories in the Ellison anthologies, but love many in the *Hall of Fame*. No problem — those "old-fashioned" stories are still very much in demand, both in the magazines and at book length.

Or you may be interested only in the hottest, most innovative entries in the current issues of the magazines. Fine — there's always room for more.

Or you may realize that *nobody* is doing anything you really care for, and your fiction is going to stand the whole field on its ear. That, too, is perfectly acceptable — you don't have to imitate anybody; it's usually better if you don't. But, having read at least a sampling of stories from every era and tradition within the field, you'll at least know what has been done before: what clichés the audience will be weary of, what expectations the audience will bring to your tale, what you have to explain, and what you can take for granted.

One warning, though. If you try to read everything so as not to repeat an idea that has already been used, you'll go mad. And even then, after your brilliant, original story has been published, some helpful reader will point out that the exact same idea was used in an obscure story by Lloyd

Biggle, Jr., or Edmund Hamilton or John W. Campbell or H. Beam Piper or . . . you get the picture.

You're reading all these stories to get a sense of how science fiction is done, not to become paranoid and decide that you can never come up with any new ideas as good as these. When I was reading Middle English romances for a graduate class at Notre Dame, I realized that almost every one of these thirteenth-century stories would make a terrific science fiction novel if you just changed the sea to space and the boats to starships.

And most science fiction novels could easily be turned into fantasy by changing starships back into ocean-going vessels. Frank Herbert's *Dune* would fit right in with the best medieval romances, if planets became continents and the spice became a source of magical power instead of a drug necessary for space navigation. There is nothing new under the sun — or beyond it, either.

The novelty and freshness you'll bring to the field won't come from the new ideas you think up. Truly new ideas are rare, and usually turn out to be variations on old themes anyway. No, your freshness will come from the way you think, from the person you are; it will inevitably show up in your writing, provided you don't mask it with heavy-handed formulas or clichés.

If there's one thing you should learn from reading all these tales, it's that, unlike many other genres, speculative fiction is not bound to follow any particular formula. There *are* a few formulas, it's true, but most stories don't follow them — or else follow them only because what may seem to be a formula is really a mythic story that has shown up in every culture where stories have been told at all.

For science fiction and fantasy are the genres in which stories can hew closest to the archetypes and myths that readers in all times and places have hungered for. That's why writers in other genres often reach for *our* tools when they have a particularly powerful story to tell, as witness Mary Stewart's Merlin books, Mary Renault's novels of the ancient Hellenic world, E. L. Doctorow's slightly fractured history, and John Irving's talking-animal figures.

Writers of mythic stories don't use "formulas"; they just tell the stories they believe in and care about. Inevitably, archetypal themes will show up again and again. But they only work if you are not aware of them; the moment you consciously treat them as formulas, they lose the power to stir the blood of any but the most naive readers.

Boundary 4: The Literature of the Strange

Having carefully explained to you that science fiction and fantasy are merely labels for (1) an arbitrary, viselike publishing category, (2) a fluid, evolving community of readers and writers, and (3) a ghetto in which you can do almost anything you like once you learn what others have already done, I will now essay a *real* definition of the terms.

This last boundary is the clearest—and probably the least accurate—definition of science fiction and fantasy:

Speculative fiction includes all stories that take place in a setting contrary to known reality.

This includes:

1. All stories set in the future, because the future can't be known. This includes all the stories speculating about future technologies, which is, for some people, the only thing that science fiction is good for. Ironically, many stories written in the forties and fifties that were set in what was then the future—the sixties, seventies, and eighties—are no longer "futuristic." Yet they aren't "false," either, because few science fiction writers pretend that they are writing what *will* happen. Rather we write what *might* happen. So those out-of-date futures, like that depicted in the novel *1984*, simply shift from the "future" category to:

2. All stories set in the historical past that contradict known facts of history. Within the field of science fiction, these are called "alternate world" stories. For instance, what if the Cuban Missile Crisis had led to nuclear war? What if Hitler had died in 1939? In the real world, of course, these events did not happen—so stories that take place in such false pasts are the purview of science fiction and fantasy.

3. All stories set on other worlds, because we've never gone there. Whether "future humans" take part in the story or not, if it isn't Earth, it belongs to fantasy and science fiction.

4. All stories supposedly set on Earth, but before recorded history and contradicting the known archaeological record—stories about visits from ancient aliens, or ancient civilizations that left no trace, or "lost kingdoms" surviving into modern times.

5. All stories that contradict some known or supposed law of nature. Obviously, fantasy that uses magic falls into this category, but so does

much science fiction: time travel stories, for instance, or invisible-man stories.

In short, science fiction and fantasy stories are those that take place in worlds that have never existed or are not yet known.

The moment I offer this definition, however, I can think of many examples of stories that fit within these boundaries yet are not considered science fiction or fantasy by *anyone*. For instance, despite some romanticizing, Felix Salten's wonderful novel *Bambi* is a brutally accurate account of the lives of deer. Yet because in his book the animals talk to each other, something that animals simply do not do, does *Bambi* become fantasy? Perhaps, after a fashion — but you'll never find it in the fantasy section of the bookstore; you'll never find it on any fantasy fan's list of his fifty favorite fantasy novels. It doesn't fall within the boundaries of the publishing category, the expectations of the community of readers and writers, or even the raw listing of what sf and fantasy writers have written.

What about *The Odyssey* and *The Iliad*? They contain magic and gods aplenty, and it's hard to imagine any contemporary reader claiming that they represent the way the world *really* was at the time of the Trojan War, yet they were composed for an audience that believed in these gods and these heroes. To taleteller and talehearer, they were poems about history and not fantasies at all; they were epic, not mythic, tales.

Indeed, there are many who would claim that my definition of speculative fiction clearly includes the Bible and *Paradise Lost*, though there are many other people today who would be outraged to hear of either being classified as fantasy.

And what do we make of Jean Auel's prehistoric romances? They certainly contradict an archaeologist's vision of the past, yet they are presented as if they correspond to reality. And what about genre-bending books like the recent *Moondust and Madness* or Jacqueline Susann's posthumously published first novel, *Yargo*? Both have spaceships and visitors from other planets, but everything else about them clearly identifies them as pure romance novels, with no hint of any knowledge or understanding of the science fiction tradition. They fit my definition — but anyone familiar with what science fiction and fantasy *really* are would repudiate them at once.

And what about horror novels? Many of the works of Stephen King are clearly fantasies — some are even science fiction — and both King and his audience would be quick to say so. Yet many other works in the horror genre don't contradict known reality in any way; they fit in the genre because they include perfectly believable events that are so gruesome or revolting that the audience reacts with fear or disgust.

Still, despite its inadequacies, my definition has its uses. For one thing, while it includes many works that really don't belong in the genre, it doesn't exclude any works that *do*. That is, your story may fit my definition and still not be sf or fantasy, but you can be sure that if your story *doesn't* fit my definition it definitely *isn't* within the genre.

Even works by established sf or fantasy writers that are included within the genre mainly out of courtesy (or force-fitting by publishers) make *some* bows, however desultory, toward fitting this definition. They at least offer the *possibility* that the story violates known reality at some point.

More important is the fact that by this definition, speculative fiction is defined *by its milieu*. The world in which the story takes place *is* the genre boundary line. If a story doesn't take the reader into an otherwise unknowable place, it isn't speculative fiction.

One of the primary appeals of all fiction is that it takes the reader into unfamiliar places. But *how* unfamiliar is it? Like chimps in the savannas of Africa, the human audience for fiction is both afraid of and attracted to strangeness. The chimp, confronted with a stranger who is not openly attacking, will retreat to a safe distance and keep watch. Gradually, if the stranger is doing something interesting, the chimp will be attracted. Curiosity overcomes fear. Or if the stranger's actions seem threatening, the chimp will flee, call for help, or try to frighten the stranger away, as fear overcomes curiosity.

Human beings also exhibit this love-fear attitude toward strangeness — for instance, we see the fear in racism, the curiosity in the way people slow down to rubberneck as they drive past an accident on the freeway. Our attitude toward strangeness is also a key element in the way we choose the stories we believe in and care about. If a tale we're reading or watching on the screen is too familiar, it becomes boring; we know the end from the beginning and switch off the set or set the book aside. Yet if it is too unfamiliar, we reject the story as unbelievable or incomprehensible. We demand *some* strangeness, but not too much.

Fortunately, no two people want exactly the same mix of strangeness and familiarity. Some are content to read the same stories over and over again, with only a few cosmetic details changed — or so it appears to those of us who don't enjoy gothics or bodice-rippers or teen romances or literary novels about writers who can't write or painters who can't paint. Others are forever searching for something new or different, so they can no longer recognize the verities contained in old familiar stories — or so it seems to those of us who don't enjoy literary experiments like those of Faulkner, Joyce, or Robbe-Grillet.

Speculative fiction by definition is geared toward an audience that wants strangeness, an audience that wants to spend time in worlds that absolutely are *not* like the observable world around them.

This is not to say that all science fiction and fantasy stories are fresh ventures into the unknown. Many readers, having once discovered a strange world that they enjoy, want to return to that same world again and again, until they're more familiar with that imaginary place than they are with the real-world town they live in. Many speculative fiction readers who came to the genre in their teens, when they hungered for strangeness and surprise and wonder, continue to read in the genre well into middle age, when they long for the repetitive or familiar — and such readers find no shortage of sf and fantasy that will deliver the right dose of nostalgia.

Yet even the most hackneyed, shopworn science fiction or fantasy tale will feel startling and fresh to a naive reader who doesn't know the milieu is just like the one used in a thousand other stories. For the intrinsic difference between speculative and real-world fiction is that speculative fiction must take place in an unknowable world. At some point, every science fiction and fantasy story must challenge the reader's experience and learning. That's much of the reason why the genre is so open to the experimentation and innovation that other genres reject — strangeness is our bread and butter. Spread it thick or slice it thin, it's still our staff of life.

Boundary 5: Between Science Fiction and Fantasy

There's one more boundary that will matter to you — the boundary between science fiction and fantasy. That's the boundary that I ran into when I tried to sell "Tinker" to *Analog*.

The division is a real one. There are writers who exclusively write one or the other; there are important differences in the way they are written. There are even differences in the audience — common wisdom has it that more males read science fiction while more females read fantasy. The result is that the quarrels between fantasy and science fiction often take on overtones of the war between the sexes. And that's only the beginning of the ugliness. Serious science fiction writers have actually published letters or articles in which they regard fantasy as somehow a threat to "good" science fiction, sometimes because fantasy seems to be crowding science fiction off the bookstore shelves, and sometimes because too many science fiction writers are being as "sloppy" or "sentimental" in their writing as fantasy writers are. Then serious fantasy writers respond with a passionate defense of their own field—and snide remarks about science fiction as an expression of the adolescent male love affair with machines.

I have found these quarrels to be almost as sad as they are funny—like bitter arguments between small children in the same family. Don't touch me. You hit me first. I hate you. You stink. The fact is that what crowds out good science fiction is bad science fiction; science fiction improves when it borrows the best techniques of fantasy, and fantasy improves when it borrows appropriate techniques from science fiction. I suppose all the arguing does no harm—but it doesn't enlighten us much, either.

Most of us who write speculative fiction turn with equal ease from fantasy to science fiction and back again. I've written both, and have found my fantasy stories to be no easier to write, no less rigorous than my science fiction; nor have I found my science fiction to need any less sense of mythic undertone or any less passionate action than my fantasy stories.

Why, then, do you even need to think about the difference? First, because fantasy and science fiction are separate publishing categories. Most book publishers who offer both kinds of speculative fiction have separate imprints for fantasy and science fiction—or at least put one term or the other on the spine. Some even maintain a separate editorial staff for each genre. And the magazines are keenly aware of the difference between science fiction and fantasy, either because they don't publish fantasy or because they have to maintain the proper balance between them in order to hold their audience.

Yet in most bookstores, fantasy and science fiction are lumped together in the same group of shelves, alphabetized by author with no attempt to separate one from the other. And they're right to do so. Those few misguided bookstores that try to have separate science fiction and fantasy sections find that most authors who have books in one section also have books in the other. This can be very confusing for would-be buyers.

"Where's the latest Xanth novel?" asks the fifteenth kid today. "I found

Piers Anthony's books in the sci-fi section, but you don't have *any* Xanth books there."

"That's because the Xanth books are *fantasy*," says the patient bookstore clerk. "They're in the *fantasy* section."

"Well that's stupid," says the kid. "Why don't you have his books *together*?"

And the kid is right. It *is* stupid. Science fiction and fantasy are one literary community; while there are many who read or write just one, there are many more who read and write both, and it's foolish to divide them in the store. After all, sf and fantasy have a largely author-driven market. While there are certainly some readers who buy sf or fantasy like Harlequin romances, picking up anything with a spaceship or an elf on the cover, there are many others who search for favorite authors and buy only their works, only rarely branching out to sample books by writers unknown to them. These readers expect to find all of an author's books together on the shelves. They don't want "a science fiction novel" or "a fantasy" — they want the latest Asimov or Edding, Benford or Donaldson, Niven-and-Pournelle or Hickman-and-Weis.

But there is a time when the division between science fiction and fantasy really matters — and that's when you're writing the story.

Here's a good, simple, semi-accurate rule of thumb: If the story is set in a universe that follows the same rules as ours, it's science fiction. If it's set in a universe that doesn't follow our rules, it's fantasy.

Or in other words, science fiction is about what *could* be but isn't; fantasy is about what *couldn't* be.

In the main, this boundary works pretty well. As rational people, we know that magic doesn't work and superstitions are meaningless. So if magic works in your story, if superstitions come true, if there are impossible beasts like fire-breathing dragons or winged horses, if djinns come out of bottles or mumbled curses cause disease, then you're writing fantasy.

You must inform your reader as quickly as possible after the beginning of your story whether it's going to be fantasy or science fiction. If it's science fiction, and you signal this to the reader, then you have saved yourself enormous amounts of effort, because your reader will assume that all the known laws of nature apply, except where the story indicates an exception.

With fantasy, however, *anything* is possible. And where anything can happen, who cares what actually occurs? I mean, if your hero can get into trouble and then wish his way out, so what? Why worry about him? Why *care*?

The truth is that *good* fantasies carefully limit the magic that's possible. In fact, the magic has to be defined, at least in the author's mind, as a whole new set of natural laws that *cannot* be violated during the course of the story. That is, if at the beginning of the story you have established that your hero can make only three wishes, you better not have him come up with a fourth wish to save his neck right at the end. That's cheating, and your reader will be quite correct to throw your book across the room and carefully avoid anything you ever write in the future.

All speculative fiction stories have to create a strange world and introduce the reader to it—but good fantasy must also establish a whole new set of natural laws, explain them right up front, and then faithfully abide by them throughout.

Having said all this, I must now point out that there are numerous exceptions. For instance, by this definition time travel stories in which the hero meets himself and stories that show spaceships traveling faster than light should all be classed as fantasy, because they violate known laws of nature—and yet both are definitely classed as science fiction, not fantasy.

Why? One explanation is that people were writing these stories as science fiction before the relevant laws of science were widely known, and so these tales remain science fiction under a sort of grandfather clause. Another explanation is that there was no commercial publishing category of fantasy until the 1960s, so a lot of fantasy came to live quite comfortably within the tent of science fiction and, when the fantasy publishing category came into existence, nobody bothered to move them from one category to the other. They were already conventional.

But to all these explanations I say "bunk." Time travel and faster-than-light (FTL) starships respect the *real* boundary between fantasy and science fiction: They have metal and plastic; they use heavy machinery, and so they're science fiction. If you have people do some magic, impossible thing by stroking a talisman or praying to a tree, it's fantasy; if they do the same thing by pressing a button or climbing inside a machine, it's science fiction.

So in a sense even science fiction stories have to define the "rules of magic" as they apply in the world of the tale, just as fantasies do. If FTL travel is possible in your science fiction universe, you have to establish that fact early on. If you want time travel, you must either make the story be *about* time travel or establish immediately that time travel is commonplace in the world of the story.

Still, the difference remains: If a story is perceived as fantasy, the reader must be told as soon as possible the "natural laws" that apply in this fantasy world, whereas if the story is perceived as science fiction, the reader will assume that the natural laws of *this* universe apply until he is told otherwise.

Note that this applies only to the beginning of the story. Your "fantasy" might end up with all seeming magic explained away as perfectly natural phenomena; your "science fiction story" might end up being a tale of witchcraft or vampirism in space. Indeed, this is exactly what Sheri Tepper did in her nine-volume *True Game* series. The story deals with people who spend their lives acting out an elaborate chesslike game, discovering and using innate magical abilities like shape-changing. Never mind that by the third volume you learn that these people are all descended from colonists who came to this planet from Earth. Don't be distracted by the conclusion, which explains in perfectly natural terms where all their seemingly magical powers come from. The story begins with a fantasy feel, so that Tepper has to unfold the laws of the universe very early in the first volume, the way a fantasy writer must.

On the other hand, David Zindell's brilliant science fiction novel *Neverness* ends up with almost as many gods and mythical, magical events as the *Iliad* and *Odyssey* combined. Yet because it begins with a science fiction feel, the reader assumes from the start that the laws of the known universe apply *with exceptions*. The book is correctly marketed as science fiction, and that's how it's received.

These are the boundaries of speculative fiction, and within that country, the boundary between science fiction and fantasy. There are high walls here and there, and high-voltage fences, and moats with alligators — but there's always a way over or under or around the obstacle. You must be aware of the boundaries; you must tread carefully whenever you get near one; but you are not their prisoner.

Indeed, you might think of the genre boundaries not as obstacles, but rather as dikes and levees that hold out the river or the sea. Wherever they are raised up, they allow you to cultivate new land; and when you need a new space to plant your story, just put up a new dike where you want it to be. If enough of us like your story, we'll accept your new boundary as the true one, and plant a few stories of our own in your new-found land. It's the best gift we can give each other. We're all of us harvesting crops in lands opened up by the pioneers in our field—Wells, Verne, Merritt, Haggard, Lovecraft, Shelley, Tolkien, and many others. But we're none of us confined to the territory they discovered. It's just the starting point.

How can we create the literature of the strange if we stay in well-mapped lands?

2. World Creation

*S*tories start working on you in a thousand different ways. I'm going to give you some personal examples, so you can see something of the process one writer goes through. The point is not that you should do it my way, but rather that there *is* no right way to come up with a story concept.

1. Where Ideas Come From

I was sixteen, and my older brother's girlfriend (now his wife) had urged me to read Isaac Asimov's Foundation trilogy (*Foundation*, *Foundation and Empire*, and *Second Foundation*). It had been years since I last read science fiction regularly, but these books so enthralled me that I wanted not only to read more science fiction, but also to try writing it. At the time I supposed that to write a science fiction story you had to come up with a futuristic idea. My older brother, Bill, was in the army, having just returned from a tour of duty in Korea, and so military thoughts were on my mind.

One day as my father was driving me to school through the bottomlands of the Provo River in Utah, I began trying to imagine what kind of war-games would be developed to train soldiers for combat in space. It would be useless to have land-based training games, since that wouldn't prepare you for three-dimensional fighting in the null-gravity environment of space. Even training in airplanes would be pointless, since there is still a definite horizontal orientation to flying in an atmosphere—straight up and straight down are very different from straight across!

So the only place where soldiers could train to think and move easily and naturally in space combat would be outside the gravity well of any planet. It couldn't be in open space—you'd lose too many trainees that way, drifting off in the midst of the game. So there had to be a huge enclosed room in a null-G environment, with variable gridworks and obstacles changing from game to game, so the trainees could simulate fighting among spaceships or the debris of battle.

I imagined that they would play with small handheld lasers, while wearing suits of body armor that would serve a double purpose—to protect them against damage from collisions during mock battles, and also to electronically record when someone scored a hit on your body. If you were hit in the leg, your leg would become immobile; if you were hit in the head or body, your whole suit would freeze. But you would remain present in the battle, drifting just like a corpse, serving as one more obstacle or bit of cover.

This was in 1968. I didn't get around to writing the story "Ender's Game" until 1975. That's because the battleroom wasn't a *story*, it was merely a setting—and not a complete milieu, either, since the soldiers training there wouldn't be in the battleroom twenty-four hours a day. There had to be a whole universe built up around the battleroom, and I was too young and inexperienced to know the questions that had to be asked.

In 1975, I asked them. Who was the enemy they were training to fight? Other humans? No, aliens—and cliché aliens at that. Bug-eyed monsters. Our worst nightmares, only now they were here in real life. And who were the trainees? Not combat soldiers, I decided, but rather people being trained to pilot starships into battle. The point was not to learn hand-to-hand combat, but rather to learn how to move quickly and efficiently, how to plan, how to take and give orders, and above all how to think three-dimensionally.

And then I asked the question that made all the difference. I knew that, having gladly missed out on combat in Vietnam, I hadn't the experience to write about the lives of *men* in combat. But what if they weren't men at all? What if they were children? What if the starships they'd be piloting were actually billions of miles away, and the kids thought they were playing *games*?

Now I had a world: humans fighting off alien invaders, with children as the commanders of their fleet. There was still a lot of work to do, but it was a simple matter to come up with my main character, the young child whose genius in three-dimensional combat in the battleroom would make him the ideal choice to command the human fleet.

Notice, though, that I didn't have even the seed of a good science fiction story until after I had a clear idea of the world in which the story would take place.

The same thing is true of fantasy. Another personal example:

I like to draw maps. That's how I doodle when other people are talking, by drawing coastlines and then putting in mountains, rivers, cities, national boundaries. Then, if the map that results intrigues me, I begin to make up more information—which nations speak the same language, what their history has been, which nations are prospering, which waning.

In 1976 I was cast in a musical comedy playing in Salt Lake City. We rehearsed in an old building downtown that was scheduled for demolition to make way for the new Crossroads Mall. In one corner of the rehearsal area there was a pile of junk—broken chairs, tilting shelves, stuff that was utterly useless. But amid the garbage I found a ream of onionskin paper of an odd size, larger than normal. I can't let paper like that go to waste! So I brought it home and saved it.

Now it's 1979. I'm living in a house in Sandy, Utah, working on the first draft of my novel *Saints*. I'm also on a radical diet losing about a billion pounds. My wife and son are down in Orem, Utah, living with her parents so they can take care of her and Geoffrey while she recovers from a miscarriage; I can't do it because I have a deadline to meet. So I'm hungry, tired, and lonely.

One night, exhausted from writing, I wander around the house and find that ream of outsize paper, saved all those years and never used. I grab a few sheets and head upstairs. The TV goes on, I lie on the bed, lay a sheet of paper atop a notebook, and begin to doodle a map while I listen to the Channel 2 news and then the Carson show.

Only this time, I doodle a different kind of map. After all, this paper cries out for something special, and I'm tired of coastlines and continents. I trace a bend in a river, and instead of dots for cities, I begin drawing tiny squares and rectangles to represent buildings, with gaps marking the streets. Heavy lines denote the walls of a castle; more heavy lines show the city walls. And I put gates in the walls.

A few nights later, the map is finished. Now it's time for naming. I had put in a few religious sites; the gate that leads into the main temple area gets the name "God's Gate." The gate near the commercial area is named "Asses' Gate" because that's the beast of burden the merchants use. One riverside gate, leading to the main street through the city, is "King's Gate";

another, near the animal stalls outside the city and leading directly to the Great Market, is "Grocers' Gate."

Then the idea occurs to me that maybe when you enter at a particular gate, you get a certain kind of pass that limits you to certain areas and activities in the city inside the wall. If you come in at one gate, you find a completely different kind of city from the one you find when you enter at another. Come in as a pilgrim through God's Gate, and you don't leave the temple area. Come in as a grocer and you have the run of the market but can't go near the trading floors.

Knowing this, I crudely named the gate near the poor section of town, with hundreds of tiny houses, "Piss Gate," because people who entered there only had a three-day pass allowing them to attempt to find work; if they remained after three days, they were imprisoned or killed or sold into slavery. A hopeless, desperate way to enter the city.

But not the *most* hopeless way. For there was one gate that, in the process of drawing, I had accidently drawn with no gap between the two towers that guarded it. Even after slightly redrawing the towers, there was no gap between them. Unless I resorted to Liquid Paper, that entrance to the city was spoiled.

Except that I believe, when it comes to storytelling—and making up maps of imaginary lands *is* a kind of storytelling—that mistakes are often the beginning of the best ideas. After all, a mistake wasn't *planned*. It isn't likely to be a cliché. All you have to do is think of a reason why the mistake isn't a mistake at all, and you might have something fresh and wonderful, something to stimulate a story you never thought of quite that way before. So I thought—what if this gate has been permanently closed off? I drew houses right across both faces of the gate. That explained why there was no gap between the towers.

Now, as I was naming all the gates, I had to wonder why this gate had been closed. And then I realized that this gate was closed because it had been the magical way into the city. A walled city spoke of medieval times; what could be more natural than to have this be the setting for a fantasy? The political powers in the city would naturally resent or fear the rival power of magicians; the gate would have been closed years ago. Only it wasn't closed completely. You can still get through, if you can pay the right bribes, but you enter the city as a criminal, with no pass at all, and the city you find is a dark, dangerous, magical one where the rules of nature don't work the way they used to.

It happened that this closed gate was near a section of town where I had drawn a small shrine that, for reasons I cannot remember, I had already named "Hart's Hope." I decided that this magical gate had once been the *main* route into the city, back when the Hart was the god of this place, long before the god called God came to be worshipped in the temple in the southeast corner. So the worshippers of the old god, the Hart, would enter town through this gateway.

Did I have a story? By no means. I still didn't even have a world. I set the map aside.

Around that time, the TV news was full of stories about a couple in Layton, Utah, who had just given birth to twins conjoined at the top of their heads. It was a tricky operation to separate them, and the photos before they were separated were disturbingly alien. But, being a perverse sort of person, I tried to imagine what could be *worse*. Not more life-threatening—simply worse to *see*. Worse to live through.

I came up with the idea of two sisters who were born joined at the face. One sister was staring directly into her twin's face; after separation, her face would be a blank mask, with no eyes, no real nose, and only a gap for a mouth. The other twin, though, was facing half away; after separation, while one eye was missing and one cheek was a ruin, her profile from the other side would look perfectly normal. Which sister suffered more, the one who would never see how hideous she was, would never look at others looking away from her? Or the one who, by turning her face just so, could catch a glimpse of how beautiful she and her sister *could* have been; and then, by staring at herself full in the face in the mirror, could see just how hideously deformed she was?

I even tried writing a story about these sisters. The draft is lost, which is just as well—it was going nowhere.

Around that time I discovered the writings of Mary Renault. When I read her book *The King Must Die*, in which the ancient Greek women have a separate, older religion which secretly rivals the public religion of the men, I realized that there mustn't be merely two rival gods in the city I had drawn—the Hart and the god named God—there must be another tradition of worship. A women's religion, and the god would be the Sweet Sisters, those two women who were born joined at the face. One of them was permanently staring inward, contemplating the inner secrets of the universe, breathing only the breath that her sister had already inhaled; while the other, seeing half in and half out, was able to see our world and communicate with her worshippers. However, at the time of my story—whatever it would be—the two sisters had been forcibly separated, thereby making it impossible for *either* to see into the mind of God. The one was blind, remembering only the sight of the infinite; the other, with her single eye, could remember only the mortal world that constantly impinged on her vision.

Who would have the power to separate these women? I thought at first that it must be the god named God, and that the Hart would eventually ally with them and rejoin them. But that would be a story about gods, and that wouldn't be interesting even to me. So instead I knew it had to be a mortal who had somehow gained enough power to tame not only the Sweet Sisters, but also the Hart and the god named God.

Did I have a story yet? No. I had a map of a fascinating city (fascinating to me, at least) and a trio—temporarily a quartet—of gods.

I began teaching a science fiction writing class at the University of Utah, and on the first day of class, when there were no stories to critique, I began a spur-of-the-moment exercise designed simply to show that science fiction and fantasy ideas are ridiculously easy to come up with. I asked questions; they improvised answers; and out of the answers, we made stories. To my surprise, the idea was not just a five-minute exercise—it became a fun, exciting session that took almost the whole period. I have since used the process in every class or workshop I've taught, and have put on a "Thousand Ideas in an Hour" session at almost every science fiction convention I've attended and every school I've visited. Not only is the process always entertaining, but also the results are always different and *always* workable as stories.

To wit: At the very first session, I asked them to think of the "price of magic." In a fantasy, if magic has no limitations, the characters are omnipotent gods; anything can happen, and so there's no story. There have to be strict limits on magic. *Dungeons and Dragons* uses a seniority system that may work well for games, but for stories it is truly stupid: The longer you manage to stay alive, the more spells you know and the more power you have. I wanted my students to come up with better limitations, and I wanted them to think of it as a price to be paid for every bit of magical power that was used.

Many ideas come up in such sessions, but one that came up the first time, which really stuck in my mind, was that the cost of magic was blood. How would that work? You wouldn't prick your own finger to get power—

that was too easy. It had to be enough blood from the creature that the creature's whole life was contained in it; you could only get the power as the creature bled to death. The *amount* of power depended on the creature whose blood you used.

You could kill a fly and get the power to keep the soup from boiling over. You could kill a rabbit and make an enemy sick or heal a child. You could kill a deer—a hart!—and have the power to be invisible for hours or days. And you could kill a man and get *real* power.

But my students were just as perverse as I was. Wouldn't you get even more power if you killed a child? After all, children have more life in them—they haven't used up so much of it. And what if you kill your *own* child? Wouldn't that give you even more power?

Yes, but what sort of person would ever do what it took to obtain such power? Ultimate power would be in the hands of monstrous people. People monstrous enough, perhaps, to separate the Sweet Sisters and imprison the Hart and the god named God.

I had the whole milieu at last. The city of Hart's Hope was being ruled by a mortal so cruel he killed his own child—no, *she* killed *her* own child—in order to gain so much power that she could bind the gods. And my hero would be the one who undid her power, not by killing another child, but by turning her own power against her. I wasn't sure how that would be done, and *wouldn't* be sure until near the end of the first draft, but I knew that my hero would have been raised up by the gods—who were not *completely* bound—to have an anti-magical power. He would be a magic sink, a person who could absorb and use up magical power without ever having the ability to use that power himself. He was a negation of power.

There was much *more* development before I was ready to write my fantasy novel *Hart's Hope*, but I knew the world in which it took place and I knew who some of my main characters were. What lay ahead was some of the most fascinating work—fleshing out the characters, discovering their unpredictable relationships with each other and with the world around them, and, finally, working out the storyline: the intersecting pathways of those characters through the world I had created.

Still, after all this planning, some of the best parts of the story came on the spur of the moment as I was writing the first draft. For instance, it never occurred to me until I found myself writing it that the god named "God" should be a feeble old man polishing woodwork in the palace of Queen Beauty; nor did any of my planning include the writing system in which words have different meanings when read forward and backward, or when interpreted as numbers. But such impromptu additions would not have been possible had I not laid down many strata of creation before I started that draft.

The Ripening Idea

The first thing you should learn from these two examples is that no two stories are developed in exactly the same way. However, in my experience one thing is constant: Good stories don't come from trying to write a story the moment I think of the first idea. All but a handful of my stories have come from combining two completely unrelated ideas that have been following their own tracks through my imagination. And all the stories I was still proud of six months after writing them have come from ideas that ripened for many months — usually years — between the time I first thought of them and the time they were ready to put into a story.

"Great," you say. "I pick up this book, hoping to learn how to write speculative fiction, and now this guy's telling me that I have to wait months or years before writing stories about any new ideas I think of."

That's what I'm telling you: You'll probably have to wait months or years before writing *good* versions of story ideas you come up with *now*. But you probably already have hundreds of story ideas that have been ripening inside you for many years. For some writers, one of the best ways to help an idea ripen is to try writing a draft of it, seeing what comes up when you actually try to make it into a story. As long as you recognize that the draft you write immediately after thinking of the idea will almost certainly have to be thrown away and rewritten from the beginning, you'll be fine.

That immediate draft — or, if you are another kind of creator, the first outlines and sketches, maps and histories, jotted scenes and scraps of dialogue — is the writer's equivalent of what a composer does when he plinks out a new theme on the piano, just to hear it. He doesn't immediately score and orchestrate the theme — first he has to play it over and over, varying it, changing rhythms, pitches, key, imagining different voices and timbres playing the theme, imagining different harmonies and countermelodies. By the time the composer actually starts to arrange and orchestrate the piece, the theme will have been transformed many times over. The first version is all but forgotten.

Some writers have to do all their inventing before they ever try to write out a narrative. Other writers have to try out the narrative immediately, then rework it over and over, letting new ideas come to them as they write each draft. I'm somewhere between the two extremes: I do a lot of outlining and planning before I write, until I feel that the story is ripe—but then, as I write, all kinds of new ideas come to me and I freely explore each new avenue that feels as if it might lead somewhere fun. As a result my novels almost never have much to do with the outlines I submit to the publishers at contract time—but since the novels are always much *better* than the outlines, the publishers haven't complained yet.

The Idea Net

The second thing you should learn from my examples is that ideas come from everywhere, provided that you're thinking about everything that happens to you as a potential story. I like to think that the difference between storytellers and non-storytellers is that we storytellers, like fishermen, are constantly dragging an "idea net" along with us. Other people pass through their lives and never notice how many stories are going on all around them; we, however, think of everything as a potential story.

And the idea net consists of three questions: "Why?" "How?" and "What result?" The first question is really two: When you ask, "Why did John slap Mary across the face?" I can answer with either the first cause, "Because she slapped him," or the final cause, "In order to show her who was boss." Both might be true at the same time. The first cause is like dominoes: Domino B fell over because Domino A fell first and pushed it. The final cause deals with purpose, with *intent*: Someone performs an action *in order to* bring about some desired result.

Both causes are acting on characters in stories all the time, and you must know answers to both kinds of "why" before you understand your characters.

In fact, to write stories that are any good at all, you have to realize that there is never just one answer to *any* of these questions. Every event has more than one cause and more than one result. When John slapped Mary, not only did she act more timidly around him, but also she resented him and constantly worked to find ways to make him suffer for having hit her.

Furthermore, John himself never realized that he was the kind of man who slapped women. Even though he excused himself by telling himself that after all, she slapped him first, it still gnawed at him that he had hit her; he felt guilty and tried to make it up to her.

Even that is too easy. Consciously, John feels guilty. Unconsciously, he's rather proud of it. He had never hit anyone in his life till now, and at the moment he struck Mary, he felt a sense of raw power that he had never felt. It made him a bit more belligerent, made him strut a little in his dealings with others. In fact, the unconscious psychological pay-off was strong enough that he will seek, without knowing it, excuses to slap and hit and push more people. Especially Mary.

And Mary's resentment and subtle rebellion are also not complicated enough to be a fair representative of reality. Perhaps it gradually dawns on her that John is becoming even *more* domineering—her only way out is to leave him. So she leaves, taking the children with her, and he, feeling completely unmanned by this, begins to follow her. He tells himself that he's trying to find her in order to make it up to her and help take care of the children; even if she doesn't want him back, he has a right to see his kids. But unconsciously, he's following her in order to beat her up again, maybe kill her—*then* she'll know who's boss.

Or perhaps Mary's unconscious reaction is completely different. Maybe she was raised by a strong father or mother who slapped the family around. Maybe she unconsciously wanted John to act out this physically domineering role, and it wasn't until she slapped him herself that he actually did what she wanted. So her subtle vengeances for his violence are really provocations. She stays with him, unconsciously hoping to continue provoking him into violence so she can fear and admire him the way she feared and admired her battering parent. Her unconscious strategy is completely successful; John finds himself hitting her more and more often. But he can't bear to be the person she is turning him into—he leaves *her*.

Or maybe they stay together and raise another generation just like them.

Or maybe there are still *more* results—and more hidden causes and motives—that will change the shape of the story. I hope you see, though, that with every variation, every new layer of cause and effect, the characters—and the story—become richer, deeper, more complex, and potentially more truthful and insightful.

This is not limited to individual characters. Nothing is sillier than a story that has some great event in the world that provokes only *one* response from society at large. Never in the history of the world has any society been perfectly unanimous in its response to any event. Nor has any innovation been introduced into the world without unpredictable side effects. When the car was invented and popularized, no one could have imagined that it would lead to the drive-in movie and the drive-up bank, to freeways and double-trailer trucks, to pollution and the greenhouse effect and the political ramifications of OPEC, and to the gathering of wealth and military power by a handful of Islamic nations, giving them influence in the world far beyond what their population and other resources would warrant.

Yet in your stories, *you* must imagine all these things, not just because it will make the world of your story more complete, but also because the very completeness of the world will transform your story and make it far more truthful. As your characters move through a more complex world, they will have to respond with greater subtlety and flexibility; the constant surprises they run into will also surprise the reader — and you!

2. Make Rules for Your World

So far, world creation sounds like a marvelous free-for-all, in which you come up with all kinds of ideas, ask "why" and "how" and "what result" a lot, and when there's a really big pile of good stuff, you sit down and write.

I wish it were that easy. But that big pile of neat ideas is just that — a pile, shapeless, chaotic. Before you can tell a meaningful story, you have to hone and sharpen your understanding of the world, and that begins with the fundamental rules, the natural laws.

Remember, because speculative fiction always differs from the knowable world, the reader is uncertain about what can and can't happen in the story *until* the writer has spelled out the rules. And you, as a writer, can't be certain of anything until *you* know the rules as well.

Rules of Starflight

Take space travel, for instance. Why would a story need space travel at all?

One reason might be simply that you want a landscape completely different from Earth. Another might be that you want your story to take place in a developing society, a *frontier* that is so far away from settled places that your characters can't call for help and expect it to come anytime soon.

But let's say your reason is even more basic. Your story centers around an alien society that you have thoroughly developed. The aliens live in an environment that is pretty much Earthlike, so that either species can live in the other's habitat. But the aliens are strange enough that there's no way they could have evolved on Earth. So you have to put them on another planet.

Other planets in our solar system just won't do. Despite speculation in earlier years, the *Voyager II* photographs seem to confirm that not only is there no planet or moon remotely suitable for Earthlike life, there isn't much chance of any kind of life at *all*. So your aliens are going to have to inhabit a planet in another star system.

This poses no problem if there are no humans in your story. If the story takes place entirely within the alien society, with no human perspective at all, then space travel plays no role in your story. But this sort of story — aliens but no humans — is fairly rare in science fiction, and for good reason. The presence of humans in a story about aliens, even if the story is told from the alien point of view, gives the reader (who is quite likely to be human) a frame of reference, a way to contrast the aliens with the humans and see exactly how the aliens are different and how this affects their society.

But if you tell the story with no humans at all, then your point-of-view characters will have to be alien, and since they have never seen a human, they cannot realistically provide a contrast. They can't even *explain* anything, unless you resort to tactics like this: "Digger-of-Holes imagined for a moment what it would be like if his eyes were on the front of his head, with overlapping vision, like the tiny shrew on the branch in front of him. How could the creature see what was happening behind it? And how could its tiny brain make sense of two overlapping but different fields of view?" This is sensible enough, but how often do you think you can get away with this before the reader gets quite impatient with a supposedly alien character who keeps thinking about things pertaining to humans that he's never seen?

(Usually, of course, such things are handled even more ineptly — by having Digger-of-Holes imagine binocular vision *without* seeing a tree-shrew, for instance — or, worse yet, having an alien scientist give a brief lecture on the benefits of binocular vision. Such techniques get the facts across, all right — but at the cost of shattering the believability of the characters and forcing the readers to be aware of how the author is manipulating the story.)

In any event, your story happens to be one that requires the presence of human beings, so you don't face the problems of the aliens-only story. However, now you *do* face the problems of travel between star systems.

Why? Your story isn't *about* space travel! At the beginning, the humans have already arrived on the alien planet (or, perhaps, the aliens have already arrived on Earth).

I assure you, though, that you *must* determine the rules of interstellar flight in your story's universe, and, at some point early in the story, you must let the reader know what those rules are. The reason for this will become clear as we go over the possible rules.

The problem of interstellar flight is two-fold: the speed of light, and the ratio of fuel mass to fuel energy.

Let's take the speed of light first. According to Einstein's theory, light-speed is the absolute ceiling on the speed of any motion in the universe. *Nothing* can go faster than light. Furthermore, anything that actually *goes* the speed of light *becomes* energy. So you can't get from one star system to another any faster than a bit more than one year per light-year of distance between them. To get from Earth to a star system thirty light-years away would take, say, thirty-one years. Your human characters, who were in their twenties when they left, are now in their fifties.

What are the strategies for getting around the lightspeed barrier?

Hyperspace. Though this goes by many different names, the idea is as old as the 1940s at least, and there's really no reason to make up a new term, since if hyperspace is ever found to exist it will almost certainly be *called* hyperspace — the way that when robots were finally created, they were *called* robots because science fiction writers had been calling artificial mechanical men by that name ever since Czech writer Karl Capek coined the term in his play *RUR* back in the 1930s. You can call it hyperspace — in fact, you probably *should* call it hyperspace, since most of your readers will be quite familiar with that term and will recognize it instantly.

Hyperspace is based on the idea that space, which seems three-dimensional to us, is really four-dimensional (or more!); and that in another dimension, *our* space is folded and curved so that locations that seem far apart to us are really quite close together, provided you can find a way to get out of our three-dimensional space, pass through hyper-dimensional space, and then come back out at the point you desire.

This passage through hyperspace is usually called "the jump," and there are many different rules associated with it. Isaac Asimov had a robot story in which the jump to hyperspace caused human beings to temporarily cease to exist, a sort of mini-death that drove a robot pilot mad trying to take humans through the jump.

Timothy Zahn's "Cascade Point" and other stories set in that same universe propose that at the moment of the jump, there is an infinite array of possible points of emergence, in most of which you die; but since it is only the jumps that you survive that you remember, you're never aware of the universes in which you are dead.

Other versions of hyperspace require that you have to be near a large star in order to make the jump, or that you *can't* be near a large gravity source or the jump gets distorted. In some stories Heinlein allows an infinite number of possible jumps, with your emergence depending on elaborately careful calculations of your velocity and trajectory leading to the jump. Others, like Frederik Pohl with his Heechee novels, have written stories allowing only a limited number of gateways through space, each leading consistently to its own destination—which, until all the gateways are mapped, might as easily be an inhabited world or the edge of a black hole.

And some versions of hyperspace don't even require a spaceship. They place "doorways" or "gates" or "tunnels" on or near a planet's surface, and if you simply walk through the right spot, going in the correct direction, you end up on—or near—the surface of another planet!

Another version of this, often used by Larry Niven, is that such doorways are not natural, but are machines that create passages through hyperspace. And in one variation of this, hyperspace isn't used at all. You get into a device that looks a bit like an old-fashioned phonebooth, which analyzes your body, breaks it down into its constituent parts, and then transmits an image of it at lightspeed to a booth on another planet (or elsewhere on Earth) that carefully reconstructs you. In either case, booths can only send you to other booths, so that somebody has to make the long journey to other planets at sub-lightspeed *first*, in order to assemble the booth that will allow others to follow them instantaneously.

The advantage of hyperspace in all its variations is that it allows relatively quick, cheap passage between worlds. How quick and how cheap is up to you. Think of it as being like voyages between the New World and the Old World. In 1550, the voyage was uncertain; some passengers and crew on every voyage died before they reached land, and some ships disappeared without a trace. By the mid-1800s, the voyage was much faster and death far less likely, though the trip was still miserable. In the age of steam, there were still wrecks and losses, but the voyage was cut down to a week or two. Today, it can take only a few hours on the Concorde. You can have starflight using hyperspace that functions at any one of these danger levels. It's as safe and fast as the Concorde—or it's as dangerous and slow and uncertain as a caravel navigating with a quadrant and an unreliable clock.

Why must you decide all these things, when your story begins after the voyage is over? First, because the characters who did the traveling—human or alien—have just finished the voyage, and their relationship with each other and their attitude toward this new world and toward authorities on the old one will be largely shaped by what the voyage back entails.

If another ship can't come for months, if the whole voyage was at risk of death and some *did* die, and if there's only a 60-40 chance of getting back home alive, then the voyagers will be determined to survive on the new planet, and will be grimly aware that if they don't make things work, their lives may end. They also won't take faraway authorities on their home planet half so seriously.

But if they reached the planet by taking a six-hour flight, and traffic between this world and the home planet will be easy and frequent, they have much less at stake, and their attitude will be far more casual. Furthermore, homeworld authorities will be much more involved, and reinforcements or replacements will be easy to obtain.

Why must you establish clearly what the rules of space travel are? So that the reader understands why the characters are getting so upset—or why they're *not* getting terribly upset—when things go wrong. So that the reader knows just what's at stake.

And—not a trivial consideration—so that the experienced science fiction reader will recognize your proper use of a standard device and feel confident that the story is being written by somebody who knows how this is done. Even if you plan to be rebellious and *not* use standard devices, you still must address the same issues; the effect on the reader is still reassuring.

Generation ships. You've decided you don't want to use hyperspace, either because it strikes you as nonsense science or because you don't want all that coming and going on your new planet. Another alternative is to send a ship at sub-lightspeed and let the voyage take as long as it takes.

Without getting into the science of it (primarily because I don't understand it in any kind of detail myself), the problem with sublight voyages is that they take a *long* time. And you have to carry all your fuel with you. The good news is that you can coast most of the way — there's little friction in space, and once you reach a certain speed, you should continue traveling at that speed in the same direction until something happens to turn you or slow you down. So most of the voyage needs no fuel at all.

The bad news is that your fuel is part of the mass that your fuel has to lift. There comes a point where the fuel to accelerate any more will add enough weight that you either can't lift it or can't design a sturdy enough ship to hold it. Furthermore, because it takes just as much fuel to slow you down at the end of your voyage so you don't just sail right on past your destination, you have to save exactly half your fuel for the slowdown, plus any fuel required for maneuvering into orbit. That means that the fuel must be able to accelerate more than twice its own mass. Worse yet, if there isn't any more fuel *at* your destination, you're either not coming home again or you're going to have to carry more than *four times* the fuel needed to accelerate you to your traveling speed.

So that you don't waste fuel trying to lift a huge ship out of the gravity well of a planet like Earth, such ships are usually assumed to have been built out in space and launched from a point as far as possible from the Sun. Thus, when they arrive at the new world, they put their huge ship into orbit and use landing vehicles or launches or (nowadays) shuttles to get down to the planet's surface.

Using the technology I've just described, you'll be lucky to get to ten percent of lightspeed. That's pretty fast — about 67 million miles an hour — but at that rate, it will take your ship more than *three hundred years* to get to a star system thirty light-years away. And that doesn't even allow for acceleration time!

That's why such ships are called "generation ships." Assuming that the ship is a completely self-contained environment, with plants to constantly refresh the atmosphere and grow food, a whole human society lives aboard the ship. People are born, grow old, and die, and the elements of their bodies are processed and returned to the ecosystem within the ship. This idea has been well-explored in many stories — particularly stories about ships where the people have forgotten their origin, forgotten even that the ship is a ship — but it has a lot of life left in it.

The problem with this (besides the fact that a completely self-contained ecosystem would be almost impossible to create) is that none of the people who reach the new world have any direct memories of their home planet. Their whole history for generations has been inside a ship—why would they even *want* to go out onto a planet's surface? The fact of living inside a ship for so long is so powerful that it almost takes over the story. If your story is *about* that, like Rebecca Brown Ore's brilliant debut story, "Projectile Weapons and Wild Alien Water," then that's fine—but if your story is about something else, a generation ship is hard to get over.

Cryo-travel. Another alternative is to have the crew travel for all those years in a state of suspended animation—either frozen or otherwise kept viable until the ship itself, or a skeleton crew, wakens the sleepers at the voyage's end. This has the advantage of not requiring living space and supplies for so many people for so many years, and it still achieves the result of making frequent voyages between the new world and the home planet unthinkable—or at least impractical.

The drawback is that if suspended animation is possible at all in your future universe, then you have to let it be used for anything it's needed for. Characters who get sick or critically injured or even killed must be rushed back to the ship and popped into a suspended animation chamber until a cure or repair can be worked out. Also, there are bound to be people who try to abuse the system to prolong their lives beyond the normal span of years. You can't have a technology exist for one purpose and then ignore it for another—not unless you want to earn the scorn of your more critical and vocal readers.

A variation on cryo-travel is to send colony ships that contain no human beings at all, but rather frozen human embryos; when the ship's computer determines that the starship has reached a habitable planet, some of the embryos are revived and raised to adulthood by computers or robots inside the ship. They come to the new planet as virtually new creations, having known neither parents nor any human society except the one they form. Obviously, this is a one-way trip with no hope of later visits or help from the home planet, since no one on the home world will even know *whether* the colony ship happened to find a habitable planet, let alone *where*.

Ramdrives. Long before the personal computer culture taught us to use the term *RAM drive* for a virtual disk in volatile memory, science fiction readers were introduced to the ramscoop stardrive, or ramdrive, that solved part of the fuel problem. Instead of carrying fuel enough to handle all of a ship's acceleration, a ramship would use conventional fuel to get up to a certain speed, then deploy a huge network like a funnel in front of it, to scoop up the loose matter that is everywhere in space. This matter would then be used as fuel, so that acceleration could continue without having to carry all the fuel along.

There are theoretical problems—the efficient use of the loose interstellar "dust," some structure for the net that isn't so heavy that the matter it collects can't provide energy enough to accelerate it, the fact that at velocities far below lightspeed the interstellar dust stops being harmless dust and starts being extremely dangerous and explosive debris that seriously harms any ship traveling that fast. But the ramdrive is fun and semi-plausible, and it allows you to have a starship that isn't the size of your average asteroid.

Time dilation. Time dilation space travel is a sort of middle path. With this set of rules, your starship can travel at a speed so close to the speed of light (say, 99.999% of lightspeed) that, while you don't turn into pure energy, you get from point A to point B at *almost* the speed of light. Relativity theory suggests that time aboard an object traveling at that speed would be compressed, so that while an outside observer might think thirty years had passed, people on the ship would only have lived through a few hours or days or weeks.

This allows you to get people from world to world without generation ships or cryo-travel. The travelers who reach the new planet have clear memories of their home world. But they won't be particularly eager to get back, because, while to them it has been only a few weeks since they left home, back there it has been thirty years. Anybody they left behind has aged a whole generation or died. And if they turned around and went back immediately, they would return home to find that someone who was twenty when they left is now eighty years old. To all intents and purposes, it's still a one-way voyage—but one that allows the travelers to arrive with their society intact, relatively unchanged by the voyage.

Still, the characters will have been cut off from anyone they knew and loved. This suggests that either the travelers will be going through some degree of grief or they will have had no close friends or family on their previous world; in either case, this will have a lot to do with how you characterize them.

And pretend not to know that to a ship traveling at such a high percentage of lightspeed, space dust would strike them like intense gamma radiation. Just say that they use a half-mile-thick layer of crushed asteroid as shielding, or that they have a force field that shields them from the radiation. Or don't say anything at all—time dilation stories are such a staple in science fiction that you really don't have to apologize for them anymore.

The ansible. I first ran across this variation on time dilation in the works of Ursula K. LeGuin, and found it one of the most useful devices in space travel. In essence, the ansible is a device that allows you to *communicate* instantaneously, regardless of distance. Thus travelers can go on one-way time-dilation voyages, yet still report to and receive instructions from people on the home planet.

This is enormously convenient if you want to have a fairly unified interstellar society and yet don't want people hopping from planet to planet the way some people commute by air from Boston to New York. A space voyage remains an irrevocable decision, cutting you off from everyone you leave behind, yet the whole interstellar society can share literature, politics, news—anything that can be transmitted by ansible. It's as if the Pilgrims could have communicated with England by radio, but still had to do all their traveling in small, dangerous, unhealthy wooden ships.

As science, of course, this is pure nonsense—yet it is so useful that many of us have used some variation on it. After all, we're not trying to predict the future, only to tell a story in a strange place!

Warp speed. I haven't even touched on the silliest of space travel rules— the one used in the *Star Trek* universe, where the speed of light is no more a barrier than the speed of sound, and you only have to persuade Scotty in the engine room to really step on the gas to get to four, eight, ten times the speed of light. This sort of stardrive shows such contempt for science that it's best to reserve it for light adventures or comic stories—or, of course, *Star Trek* novelizations.

In fact, unless you're actually writing a *Star Trek* novel (which means you must already have a contract with the publisher licensed by Paramount Pictures) or are deliberately trying to be funny, *never* refer to "warp speed" in your fiction. It's not only bad science, it also pegs you instantly as a writer who knows science fiction only through *Star Trek*. Beware of *anything* that makes non-Trekkie readers think of *Star Trek*. That's the equivalent of applying for a position as a physics professor with a résumé that lists your training as "Watched every episode of Mr. Wizard." You may actually know something, but it'll be hard to get anyone to take you seriously long enough to find out.

What the Rules Can Do for You

All this attention to space travel, and your story doesn't have a single scene aboard the ship! Do you really have to go through all this?

Yes—in your head, or perhaps in your outline. Just enough time to make your decisions about the rules and then make sure your whole story doesn't violate them. But your *reader* doesn't have to go through all that with you. Once you've decided that you're using a difficult, dangerous hyperspace where the emergence points can shift by parsecs without warning, then all you have to do is drop some reference into the story—perhaps a single sentence, like this:

"It was a perfect flight, which is to say that they didn't emerge from the jump through hyperspace in the middle of a star or heading straight for an asteroid, and even though everybody puked for days after the jump, nobody died of it."

That's it. That's all. No more discussion about the mechanics of starflight. But your readers will understand why none of the travelers is eager to leave the planet, and why it'll be quite a while before another ship comes. And now, with the rules established, you're free to do things like having your viewpoint character think of someone else this way:

> Back at Moonbase, Annie had thought Booker looked pretty good, thought he might be worth getting to know a little better. But after the hyperjump she had had to clean up his vomit while he whimpered and cried in the corner. He didn't emerge from his hysteria till they were in orbit around Rainbird. Annie knew that Booker couldn't help it, that a lot of people reacted that way to the jump, but then, she couldn't help it, either, that it was impossible to respect him anymore after that.

Maybe this relationship will be important in your story; maybe it won't. But if you didn't *know* that people puke a lot after the hyperspace jump, if you hadn't worked out the rules in advance, then you couldn't have given Annie this memory and this aspect to her relationship with Booker. The rules you establish don't limit you; they open up possibilities.

Know the rules, and the rules will make you free.

Time Travel

You have to go through the same process with time travel. Without going into the same detail, let me just list some of the possible variations on time travel.

1. If you go back in time, you can make any changes you want in the past and you'll continue to exist, because the very act of traveling in time takes you outside the timestream and removes you from the effects of changes in history. (See Asimov's *The End of Eternity*.)

2. If you go back in time, you *can* make changes that destroy your own society — so time travel is a closely guarded secret, and those who travel in time are only the most skilled and trusted people. Perhaps they are sent to rescue great works of art that have been lost for centuries. Or perhaps, as in John Varley's classic "Air Raid" (published under the pseudonym Herb Boehm), these time travelers are rescuing people from airplanes that are about to crash or ships that are about to go down with no survivors, so they can force these healthy people to colonize planets and save humanity from extinction in a hideously polluted future.

3. If you go back in time far enough, any changes you make won't have major effects in your own time, because history has a kind of inertia and tends to get itself back on track. So if you kill Napoleon as a baby, France still has an early-nineteenth-century empire and a protracted war with England, and by 1900 everything is right back where it would have been.

4. If you go back in time, you are only *able* to make changes that have no long-term effects, since any universe in which you change your own future could not exist.

5. When you go back in time, you're invisible and unable to affect anything. But you can *watch* — so there's quite a tourist business.

6. Time travel consists of going back into the *mind* of somebody living in the past, seeing events through his eyes. He doesn't know you're there. (But, in Carter Scholz's brilliant short story "The Ninth Symphony of Ludwig von Beethoven and Other Lost Songs," the presence of time-traveling observers in Beethoven's mind drove him mad and eventually killed him, stopping him from writing his greatest works.

46

The time travelers never realized what they were doing, however, because with history altered, they "knew" that Beethoven had never written any such symphonies after all.)

7. Time travel consists of going back into your *own* mind at an earlier stage in your life, able to observe but not to act. Or, in a variation, you *can* act, but then your youthful self will have no memory of what you did while your future self was in control. I used that one in a love story called "Clap Hands and Sing."

8. Time travel consists of observation only, like watching a hologram or a movie. You aren't actually there, and perhaps you aren't altogether sure that what you're seeing is the real past. Maybe it's never the same way twice! (I actually don't remember seeing a story about that—feel free to use that set of rules and see what develops.)

9. Your body remains inside the time-travel device, but a semi-real body is assembled for you in the past; your consciousness remains with that simulacrum until it dies or fades, whereupon you wake up and emerge from the machine. In a story called "Closing the Timelid," I had a group of thrillseekers using such a machine in order to go through repeated deaths by making their simulacra commit suicide.

Do you get the idea? Each one of these sets of rules opens up a whole new range of story possibilities—and trust me, there are hundreds of variations that nobody's tried yet, or that have many, many stories left in them.

The Rules of Magic
In workshops and conferences over the past decade, I've seen groups of writers and readers come up with hundreds of ways that magic might work within a fantasy society. But the basic idea is only the beginning. With magic, you must be *very* clear about the rules. First, you don't want your readers to think that *anything* can happen. Second, the more carefully you work out the rules, the more you know about the limitations on magic, the more possibilities you open up in the story.

Let's take, as an example, one of the ideas that commonly crops up in the fantasy part of my thousand-ideas sessions: The price of magic might be the loss of parts from the human body. It's simple, it's painful, and it's grotesque to imagine—sounds like a great idea to me. And there are as many variations here as there were with time travel. Here are several different ways you might turn this idea into a useful magic system:

1. When the magic user casts a spell, he loses bits off his own body, always starting with the extremities. He's never sure quite how much he's going to lose. Inevitably, however, missing fingers or hands or feet or limbs begin to be taken in society as a sign of great power — so that young people who wish to seem formidable pay to have fingers and, sometimes, limbs removed, with scars artfully arranged to look like those that magicians have. It's hard to tell who really has power and who only seems to. (Your story might be about somebody who refuses to mutilate himself; he's universally regarded as a powerless coward. Which, in fact, he is — until there comes a time when a spell is needed to save his city, a spell so powerful that *only* a person with his entire body intact can cast it — and the spell will use up all his limbs at once. Does he do it? If so, why?)

2. The magic user must actually cut off a part of his own body, or have it cut off, casting the spell while the bone is being incised. The longer he endures the pain and the larger the section of his body being removed, the more power he obtains. A whole profession of Removers would spring up, people skilled at the excruciatingly slow removal of limbs, using drugs that, while they don't dull the pain, do allow the magician to remain lucid enough to perform the spell. (Here's a chance for an interesting twist on a science fiction staple: a future society devoted to "harmless" recreational drugs. Why not have a Remover who goes into the underground apothecary trade, selling the drugs to people who just want the heightened mental effects? What will the magicians do to him then?)

3. The magic user does not have to cut off his *own* body part; he can cut off somebody else's. Thus magicians keep herds of human beings — social rejects, mental defectives, and so on — to harvest their limbs for power. In most places this practice would be illegal, of course, so that their victims would be concealed or masquerade as something else. (A good horror story using this magic system might be set in our contemporary world, as we discover people living among us who are secretly harvesting other people's limbs.)

4. The magic user can only obtain power when someone else *voluntarily* removes a body part. Thus magic is only rarely used, perhaps only at times of great need. If a private person wishes to hire a spell done, he must provide not only payment to the wizard, but also a part of his body. And at a time of great public need, the hero is not the wizard,

but the volunteer who gives up part of his body so the spell can be cast to save the town. (How about a psychological study of a pair of lovers, one a magician, the other a voluntary donor, as we come to understand why the one is willing to give up his or her body parts for the other's use?)

5. When the magician casts a spell, *someone* loses part of his body, but he can't predict who. It has to be someone known to him, however, someone connected to him in some way. And, while wizards all know this dark secret of their craft, they have never told anyone, so that nobody realizes that what causes limbs to wither up and fall off is really not a disease, but rather the wizard up the street or off there in the woods or up in the castle tower. (And here's the obvious variation: What if some common but nasty disease in our world is really the work of secret magicians? That's why certain diseases go in waves: twenty years ago it was bleeding ulcers; now it's colon cancer. And the hero of our story is a wizard who is trying to stop the suffering he and others like him are causing.)

6. When a wizard casts a spell, body parts wither and fall off the person he loves the most. The love can't be faked; if he loves himself most, it is himself who loses body parts. The greater the love, the greater the power—but also the greater the suffering of the wizard when he sees what has happened to the person he loves. This makes the most loving and compassionate people the ones with the most potential power—and yet they're the ones least likely to use it. (Here's a monstrous story idea: The child of loving parents who wakes up one morning without a limb and, seeing her devoted father getting paid, begins to suspect the connection between her maiming and his wealth.)

You get the idea. There are at least this many permutations possible with every other source of magic I've ever heard of. And the stories you tell, the world you create, will in many ways be dependent on the decisions you make about the rules of magic.

3. Invent the Past

Worlds don't spring up out of nothing. However things are now, they used to be another way, and somehow they got from there to here.

Evolution

Whenever you invent an alien creature, you should invest a great deal of effort in determining *why*, in evolutionary terms, its unusual features would have developed. Not that you have to figure out the exact mechanism of evolution — we're still arguing about that in the real world! — but you do have to think about why the alien's unusual features would have survival value.

For instance, take some aliens that were developed in a thousand-ideas session at the World Science Fiction Convention in New Orleans in 1988. I always start the alien-building part of the session by asking, "How do these aliens differ from human beings?" I reject the obvious similes: "They're like cats." "They're like dogs." I insist on something truly strange.

This time someone said, "They don't communicate by speaking."

I immediately insisted that I didn't want to deal with telepathy. "Find another way that they communicate."

There were many good suggestions, but one that worked especially well was the idea that they lived in water and communicated by passing memories directly, in chemical form, from one alien's body to another. In fact, the memory of a particular incident would replicate like the DNA of dividing cells, so that after they traded memories, each person would remember the incident as if it had happened to him.

Such a society would have no need of writing anything down, or of language at all — indeed, individual identity would be much less important to them than to us. And death would be almost meaningless. As long as you passed memories before you died, then everything you thought and experienced would continue to live on, so that even though *you* might cease to take part, everyone in the community would clearly remember having done everything you did!

Someone in the group objected that they would eventually overload, remembering everything that had ever happened to everybody who had ever lived. So we decided that there had to be a mechanism for forgetting — but not irretrievably. We imagined that they would have developed a way of encoding memories in solid form, building them into structures, perhaps even large edifices composed entirely of memory; and there would be many aliens whose sole job was to remember where memories were stored — librarians, in other words.

But why would such an ability evolve? We decided that this alien species of underwater creatures was fairly weak-bodied and not too fast, with many large, quick predators that often killed them. The tribes that survived were those that learned to manipulate rocks and corals and build shelters, or those that learned to consciously reshape their bodies into other forms—or, perhaps, those that learned to join their bodies together into large, intimidating shapes. Each tribe had a different strategy, but it could never be passed from tribe to tribe. Now, though, let's say that the subspecies that has learned to join their bodies into large forms also passes chemicals, quite accidently, from body to body while joined. And some of those chemicals are memories.

Now let's say that the rush of new memories is like a drug, a rapturous experience. Aliens begin to seek it frequently, not just waiting until they're threatened. (Perhaps the pleasure comes from the fact that the joining behavior was always triggered by fear and immediately followed by safety and relief.) There is no particular advantage to random joining of memories—these creatures aren't all *that* bright yet—except that young aliens whose parents conjoin with them and pass memories to them gain a competitive advantage over other youngsters who remain ignorant of their parents' memories.

The result is that memory-passing is strongly reinforced from generation to generation, and in true Lamarckian fashion, learned behaviors become part of the heritage of each succeeding generation. In addition, since this developed among the shape-formers, these underwater creatures would continue the habit of joining into strange shapes.

It was a terrific basis for an alien society, with a lot of story possibilities. Then, only a week later, I found myself in Gaffney, South Carolina, talking with Jim Cameron about the novel version of his movie *The Abyss*. His script was brilliant, but an area he had neglected—and properly so—was the aliens. There wasn't time or means in the film to explain them. But in the book version that I was writing, they *had* to be explained.

So I wrote an exploratory chapter (which never showed up in the book) from the point of view of the individual creature who became the original alien colonizer of Earth. I found that everything we had come up with in that thousand-ideas session in New Orleans was wonderfully useful. It was an evolutionary skeleton on which I could hang all the strange behavior of the aliens in the film.

In fact, those are probably the best aliens I've ever devised for any of my science fiction, and one of the reasons they were better than usual is because I had two unrelated idea sources: the idea session and the movie script, which provided all kinds of anomalous behavior that had to be explained. Out of the tension between the filmscript and the evolutionary path traced in that idea session there grew what seemed to me to be a truly complex, believable, and interesting alien society.

You may think that you want the aliens in your story to remain strange and mysterious, but I assure you that you won't accomplish this by skipping the step of developing their evolutionary history. If you don't know why they are what they are, why they do what they do, then the result in your story will be mere vagueness. But if you know exactly why they do what they do, you'll develop their behavior with far more precision and detail; you'll come up with many surprising twists and turns, with genuine strangeness. You'll lead your readers to the brink of understanding why the aliens do what they do; the mystery comes from the fact that the reader is never quite sure. But *you* are sure.

Read enough science fiction, and you can almost always tell the difference between the writer who has done the development and the writer who's faking it.

History. Even when you're working entirely with human societies, a vital part of world creation is knowing the history of the communities in the story. You can't just put a demagogic preacher in your town, leading a mob of self-righteous church people into a book-burning frenzy; the result is invariably caricature. Instead, take the time to figure out *why* these people are following the preacher, why they trust him and believe in him.

Don't settle for the cheap answer, either—"Because they're a bunch of dumb bigots" doesn't make for honest fiction. They may be acting like a mob in the climax of your story, but until that time they were all individuals, all different from each other, following that preacher for their own reasons.

Part of the reason is that he's charismatic. But what does "charisma" mean? Think of some specific events that must have happened. For instance, the reason Mick and Janna would follow Reverend Bucky Fay to hell and back is because when their baby was sick, he came into their home and looked into the baby's eyes and then cupped the baby's head in his hands and said, "I see you're only a few weeks gone from the presence of Jesus, and he sent you into this world to do a great work. Satan has filled your body with disease, but you are such a magnificent glorious spirit that you have the power to fight it off within you—if you want to. But I can't ask you to heal yourself, no sir. You can sense all the evil in the world, and you're so good and pure that I don't blame you if you decide not to live here a moment longer. But I beg you to stay. We need you."

The baby died a few days later, but instead of blaming Bucky Fay for not healing the infant, Mick and Janna felt sure that their baby was so good that it simply couldn't bear to live in this wicked world. They tell the story to others, and because they speak with such fervency and belief, others believe them, too. Half their identity is based on the fact that God once chose them to be parents of one of his most perfect children; if they ever doubted Bucky Fay's spiritual insights, it would be like desecrating their lost baby's grave.

Now, maybe you won't even use an incident like that in the story. But you *know* it, and because it's there in the history of that town, the people in that mob are no longer strangers to you, no longer puppets to make go through the actions you want them to perform. They've come alive, they have souls — and your story will be richer and more truthful because of it.

Biography. You'll also know more about Reverend Bucky Fay, too. You'll have pieces of his biography. And when it comes to fiction, biography isn't just a matter of filling out a résumé — when was he born, how did he do in school, what did he get his degree in, is he married or single or divorced? What matters with fiction is *why*.

Why did Bucky Fay ever go into the ministry? Was he once a believer? When he does things like that scene with Mick's and Janna's baby, does he believe, or half-believe, the things he's saying? Or does he think of these people as unbelievably dumb suckers? Or is he consumed with guilt? Or has he come to believe that he has the power to "see" things about other people, simply because everybody else believes what he says? Maybe this is how prophecy felt to Moses, he says to himself. Maybe he just kind of made stuff up, only whatever came to mind turned out to be true because God was in him.

The more you know about what has happened in a character's past *and why*, the more complex and interesting the world of your story will be. The people, the societies, all will seem real.

4. Language

How does each community within your story speak? If you have people from more than one nation, they might well speak different languages; if they're from different worlds, they certainly will.

Perhaps there's a lingua franca, a trading language like Pidgin in the Pacific, or Swahili in East Africa, or English in India, that few speak as their native tongue, but everyone speaks well enough to communicate with each other. Some writers go so far as to actually *create* the various languages — look at Tolkien's *Lord of the Rings* — but you don't really need to do that.

In fact, you probably shouldn't. For one thing, you're likely to embarrass yourself. Not many of us are gifted and deeply educated linguists like Tolkien, whose fictional languages sound so real in part because they're all based, however loosely, on real human languages.

New Words for New Meanings

Nothing is more tacky than to have a bunch of foreign-sounding words thrown into a story for no better reason than to have something that sounds foreign. James Blish called such needlessly coined words "shmeerps." If it looks like a rabbit and acts like a rabbit, calling it a *shmeerp* doesn't make it alien.

If *mugubasala* means "bread" then say *bread*! Only use the made-up stuff when it is used for a concept for which there *is* no English word. If your viewpoint character *thinks* that *mugubasala* is nothing but bread, then later discovers that it is prepared through a special process that releases a drug from the native grain, and that drug turns out to be the source of the telepathic power that the natives are suspected of having, then you are fully justified in calling the bread *mugubasala*. It really *is* different, and deserves the added importance that a foreign name bestows.

In Portuguese there's a common idiomatic expression based on the verb *dar*, to give. You ask someone, "Será que dá p'ra entrar?" and he answers, "Não dá." A literal transation would be "Will it give to enter?" and the answer means "It doesn't give." But that conveys none of the sense. When you say "Does it give?" to do something, it means "Is it possible? Is it proper? Is it right? Will it be resisted? Is it safe?" Yet not one of these terms actually conveys the precise meaning. In fact, in English there *is* no word or expression that conveys that exact meaning.

Your invented languages *should* have concepts that just can't be translated, not so that you can toss in cool-sounding phrases like "Hlobet mesh nay beggessahn dohlerem," but rather so that you can develop — and the reader can understand — the cultural and intellectual differences between cultures.

But don't leave those phrases untranslated. The commonly accepted way to handle this is to repeat the foreign phrase in English immediately afterward — provided your viewpoint character understands the language.

> *"Eu só queria tomar cafezinho," I said. All I wanted was a little coffee.*

Indeed, you never actually have to use the foreign language itself to convey the same effect. After all, presumably you're translating *all* the dialogue and narration of all your stories that aren't set in contemporary English-speaking society — so why arbitrarily choose a few words to leave untranslated, especially if the word isn't important to the story?

> *"God give me strength not to kill you for having seen my ugliness," he said to me.*
>
> *I blinked once, then realized that he was speaking Samvoric and had given me the ritual greeting between equals. I hadn't heard Samvoric in a long time, but it still sounded more natural to me than Common Speech. "God forgive me for not blinding myself at once after having beheld your glory," I said.*
>
> *Then we grinned and licked each other's cheeks. He tasted like sweat. On a cold day like this, that meant he'd either been drinking or working hard. Probably both.*

There's not one made-up word in the whole paragraph (except for the name of the language, of course), and yet you definitely get the idea that you're dealing with a foreign language — a whole foreign culture, in fact.

(If you *are* using a known foreign language, by the way, take the time and effort to get it right. Among your readers there will always be someone who speaks that language like a native. If you get it wrong, those readers lose faith in you — and rightly so. Wherever you *can* be truthful, you *should* be truthful; if your readers can see that you're acting by that credo, they'll trust you, and you'll deserve their trust. But if they catch you faking it, and doing it so carelessly that you can easily be caught, they'll figure that if the story wasn't worth much effort to you, it shouldn't be worth much to them, either. They may still like the story, but you have blunted the edge of their passion.)

Can the Human Mouth Pronounce It?

Be careful, too, that the language you invent is pronounceable for your English-speaking readers. Words or names that are mere collections of odd letters, like *xxyqhhp* or *h'psps't* are doubly dumb, first because they constantly distract the reader and force him to withdraw from the story and think about the letters on the page, and second because even strange and difficult languages, when transliterated into the Roman alphabet, will follow Roman alphabetic conventions.

If you doubt it, look at how languages as diverse as Chinese, Navaho, Arabic, Greek, and Quechua are represented in Roman characters. They're meaningless to those who don't speak the language, and when you pronounce them as written, they won't sound much like the real language, either. But you *can* pronounce them, after a fashion. And therefore they don't distract from the story, but rather help the world of the story seem more real and complete.

This especially applies to alien and foreign names. You want that name to be an instant label for a character or place—but you must remember that it can't be a merely *visual* label. Even though most of your readers don't move their lips, you must take into account the fact that many (if not most) readers have a strong oral component to their reading. In our minds, we're reading aloud, and if we run into a word or name that can't be pronounced, it stops us cold. The visual symbols—the letters—are continuously translated into the sounds of the spoken language in our minds. And for those of us who read that way, names like Ahxpxqwt are perpetual stumbling blocks.

Subsets of English

Most of the time, though, the made-up languages in your story will all be English. Or, rather, a subset of English.

Every community develops jargon—words that have meaning within the context of that community, but have no meaning, or different meanings, to outsiders. Anthony Burgess's *A Clockwork Orange* is an extreme example of this, as the reader is almost overwhelmed by the strange and at-first-incomprehensible slang of the street hoodlums. Yet so artfully designed is his future street slang that in fact you grasp the meanings of most expressions intuitively, and quickly learn the others from context. Within a few pages you think you've been speaking this slang all your life.

But Burgess is better than most of us—his invented slang is so effective because he actually understands the many mechanisms by which slang develops: circumlocution, euphemism, rhymes, irony, foreign borrowings, and many, many more. When he had his characters use the word *horror-show* for "really neat," he was, in part, following the same path that, years later, led to the use among American black youths of the word *bad* to mean "really neat."

You don't have to go to Burgess's extremes in order to use made-up languages effectively — indeed, you probably shouldn't. Invented languages are a lot more fun to make up than they are to wade through in a story. Most of the time, you'll use just a few terms to *imply* a jargon or slang or cant, just as you use only a few phrases to establish that two characters are speaking a known foreign language.

5. Scenery

This is the part that most people think of when they talk about world creation: coming up with a star system and a planet and an alien landscape. You calculate the diameter and mass of the planet, its periods of rotation and revolution, its distance from the sun, its angle of inclination, any satellites it might have, the brightness of the sun, its age.

The result is a very precise set of measurements: the surface gravity; the surface temperature; whether or not there's an atmosphere and, if there is one, what it's made of and what the prevailing winds are like; the climate in various regions of the planet; its oceans and continents (if any); tides; and, finally, the likelihood of life and the kind of life it would have.

The result can range from fairly simple things — low-gravity planets with very tall trees and animals; fast-spinning planets with high winds and very short day-night cycles; planets that don't rotate at all, so that life is only possible in a very narrow band — to complex systems that give rise to a whole novel's-worth of possibilities.

A couple of examples. Robert Forward's novel *Dragon's Egg* came from a very simple proposal: What kind of life might emerge on the surface of a neutron star? The result was one of the best pure-science novels ever written, in which the coming of an exploratory starship from Earth, first seen as a light in the sky, gives rise to the first stirrings of intelligence and curiosity among the rudimentary life forms on the neutron star's surface. Yet because the star spins so fast and time flows so swiftly for these flat, heavy creatures, by the time the human starship actually arrives, these aliens we inadvertently created have already developed spaceflight and have advanced past our primitive technological level.

Indeed, Forward is the epitome of the "hard" science fiction writer. Himself a physicist of some note, Forward's approach to fiction is almost entirely from the scientific angle. Though he's a fine storyteller, the story is always the servant of the scientific idea.

And for a large group of readers and writers of science fiction, this is the only correct approach to the field. Their preference is for the hard sciences: physics, chemistry, astronomy, geology. They consider zoology and botany to be rather suspect, and as for the "sciences" of sociology, psychology, anthropology, and archaeology, it is to laugh — to them, the social sciences are just subsets of history, an art more literary than evidentiary, speculative rather than measurable.

To hear some hard-sf people talk, you'd think they invented science fiction and all these writers of anthropological or literary or adventure sf are all johnny-come-latelies. Alas, it is not so — anthropological and literary and adventure sf all pre-date hard sf. But for a long time, starting with John W. Campbell's editorship of *Astounding* magazine, the hard stuff, the stories that took science very, very seriously, were the very best work being published in the field. The cutting edge.

Today the cutting edge has moved on — it always does — but more than any other kind of science fiction, hard sf has maintained a core of loyal supporters. *Analog* magazine, while no longer the leading publication when award time comes around, still has a larger circulation than any of the other fiction-only magazines, even though its stories fall into a very narrow subset of the field. Indeed, *Analog* seems to be the only magazine that regularly publishes formula stories, but the formulas work within the hard-sf tradition:

1. Independent thinker comes up with great idea; bureaucrats screw everything up; independent thinker straightens it all out and puts bureaucrats in their place. (This story appeals to scientists and their fans because it is a reversal of the pattern in the real world, in which scientists generally prosper according to their ability to attract grant money from bureaucrats, a relationship that forces scientists, who see themselves as an intellectual elite, into subservience.)

2. Something strange is happening; independent thinker comes along and after many false hypotheses, finally discovers the surprising an-

swer. (This formula is a reenactment of the scientific method, but endowed with far more drama than scientists ever experience in real life.)

3. A new machine/device/discovery is being tested; something goes wrong and it looks like everybody's going to die; then, after mighty efforts, either everybody dies (tragedy) or everybody lives (happy ending).

Under the editorship of Stanley Schmidt, this approach seems to be inexhaustible, and it is impossible to argue with *Analog's* circulation figures compared to the other sf-only magazines. However, while the hard-sf audience remains loyal, the rest of the field has passed on by. The only stories to rise out of *Analog* and attract attention in the field at large are the ones that either *don't* follow these formulas or transcend them.

What separates the best hard-sf writers from the run-of-the-mill ones is the fact that while the ordinary guys usually invent the scenery of their created world and maybe work up a good evolutionary track for the life forms there, they then resort to clichés for everything else. Characters, societies, events—all are taken straight out of everything else they've ever read. That's why formulas are resorted to so often.

That's why one of the most annoying things about *Analog* fiction—annoying to me, at least—is the way that most stories there show little knowledge of fundamental human systems. Writers who wouldn't dream of embarrassing themselves with a faulty calculation of atmospheric density don't even notice when their characters—whether scientists, government leaders, or gas station attendants; men or women; young or old—all talk and act and relate with other people like smart-mouth schoolboys.

The irony is that the prevalence of bad fiction in the hard-sf subgenre has led many to think that hard science fiction, by its nature, *must* be bad. Indeed, some of the great writers in the field, who first became famous during the heyday of Campbellian hard science fiction in the 1940s and 1950s, have suffered a bit of tainting by association with their supposed successors in hard sf in recent years.

What we should learn from the bad writing so common in hard-sf circles today is not that hard sf can't be written well—we have Asimov and Clarke, Niven and Clement, Sheffield and Forward to prove otherwise—but rather that there is a tremendous opportunity in the area of hard science fiction for talented, skilled storytellers who have also mastered enough of the hard sciences to speak to this audience. The audience does not insist on bad writing, merely on good science; if they are offered good science *and* good writing, they almost invariably provide such an author with a very long, secure, and well-paid career.

On the other hand, many of us who write "soft" (anthropological or sociological), literary, or adventure science fiction have made the mistake of shunning the precise sciences in our storytelling. Most of us skip the whole issue by setting all our stories on planets "very much like Earth" or on worlds that have already been fully invented by other writers. Just like the weakest of the hard-sf writers, we concentrate only on the things that interest us—social structures, elegant prose, or grand romantic adventures—and completely ignore what doesn't. To the extent that we who are now the mainstream of science fiction ignore the hard sciences in our world creation, we are as guilty of shallowness as the hard-sf writers who pay no heed to social systems, characters, and plots.

There are some writers who have done it all at once. Larry Niven, for instance, is known as one of the great hard-sf writers—but I, for one, am of the opinion that he is a leading writer in our field because he is one of the best and clearest *storytellers* we've ever had. He works in the hard sciences to create his worlds and generate his ideas—but what makes him one of our great writers is the quality of the tales that he tells within those worlds.

Perhaps the most notable recent example of fiction that does it all is Brian Aldiss's brilliant and ambitious Helliconia trilogy: *Helliconia Spring*, *Helliconia Summer*, and *Helliconia Winter*. Conceived and executed as a Great Work, the entire story takes place on a planet that orbits two binary stars. Not only is there a fairly normal annual cycle of seasons, but also there is a thousand-year cycle of super-seasons. As the planet draws near to the larger star, the overall climate becomes almost unbearably hot; as it recedes, warmed only by the smaller, cooler star, the planet becomes so cold that it almost completely freezes over. All life on the planet, including human life and society, has adapted to the millennial cycle.

As literary, anthropological, and romantic science fiction the trilogy is unexceptionable; it is also excellent hard science fiction. Most of this is due to Aldiss's genius and to his unflagging integrity as a storyteller; part, though, is surely due to the fact that he is British, not American, and Britain has largely escaped the ghettoizing process that has long afflicted American letters. Not only is science fiction itself not so firmly subdivided, nor sf so thoroughly split from fantasy, but also the whole speculative fiction field is viewed by the British literary mainstream as a legitimate area for a "real" writer to venture into. After all, it was Britain that produced H. G. Wells, Aldous Huxley, and George Orwell, honoring them as great British writers, not just as great British writers of science fiction. Thus Aldiss — like many other British writers — has remained immune to the insularity that so often makes American writers of speculative fiction use only a fraction of the tools available to storytellers.

So, if you have a bent toward hard science fiction, I urge you to broaden your scope and expect all your stories to be good fiction as well as good science. And even if you have little interest in hard science fiction, I urge you to broaden your scope and explore the possibilities that the hard sciences offer to the storyteller. And even if you know nothing about the hard sciences — even if you think you want only to write fantasy — I suggest that you get your first overview of the sciences by reading as much fiction by the great hard-sf writers of the forties, fifties, and sixties as you possibly can. You'll come out marvelously entertained — with a good survey of what the cutting edge of science was at the time each story was written.

I firmly believe that a good storyteller's education never ends, because to tell stories perfectly you have to know everything about everything. Naturally, none of us actually achieves such complete knowledge — but we should live as if we were trying to do so. You can't afford to close off any area of inquiry. Writing the same book, I recently called upon ideas I learned from reading Robert Caro's biography of Lyndon Johnson, *The Path to Power*; the detailed reference work on medieval village society, *The Lost Country Life*; Rafael Sabatini's romance *Captain Blood*; Clifford Geertz's *Interpretation of Cultures*; and Plato's *Symposium*. Who knows how much better my novel might have been had I only read a half dozen other books, or examined a dozen other subjects that I'm still hopelessly ignorant of?

In creating the strange milieu in which your story takes place, you must first understand as well as you possibly can the familiar milieu in which your own life is taking place. Until you have examined and comprehended the world around you, you can't possibly create a complex and believable imaginary world.

Indeed, one of the greatest values of speculative fiction is that creating a strange imaginary world is often the best way to help readers see the real world through fresh eyes and notice things that would otherwise remain unnoticed. Speculative fiction is not an escape from the real world, and writing it is not a way to have a literary career without having to research anything! Speculative fiction instead provides a lens through which to view the real world better than it could ever be seen with the natural eye.

In other words: You can't know too much.

3. Story Construction

*Y*ou have your world, so deep and rich that you can hardly wait to get started with the story itself. The trouble is that you don't know yet what's supposed to happen in the story. In fact, you don't even know whom the story's about.

Sometimes this isn't the problem—sometimes it's the character you think of first, and the world creation comes after. Sometimes you already know the whole story.

Or do you? The process of world creation should have changed many aspects of your main character, just as character development changes the world. At some point you began to wonder why your main character ever came to this place. (That's where many of the best ideas come from— sitting around wondering about why things are the way they are in your fictional world.) As you thought of answers to that question, you decided that she has a family, including a younger sister that she's always been jealous of, and the reason she first left her home world for this colony was to get away from her sister. Now her sister has arrived in the colony—as the administrator in charge of the very program your character works in!

Your basic story outline may well remain the same: Your main character, Jia, discovers that the desert scavengers on this planet, called scabs, are actually sentient (literally "sensible" or "feeling") creatures deserving protection. Yet at the same time, her team of xenobiologists has succeeded in developing a biobomb that will wipe out the scabs to save the colony's crops. Nothing in your world creation has caused you to change this basic story.

But now everything is complicated by the fact that it's Jia's younger sister, Wu Li, who will make the final decision about deploying the plague that will exterminate the scabs. The story is now pulling the reader along in two ways at once: The reader cares about saving an endangered people, the scabs; and the reader sympathizes with Jia's family problems, and how hard it will be for her to swallow her pride.

In your original idea, you figured that Jia's team leader was the kind of martinet who went by the book and refused to consider the idea that the scabs were sentient. It was time to deploy, so the team leader was going to deploy. This sort of stock villain is a serviceable device for moving a plot along, but there's nothing there to interest the reader. Now that the team leader is Wu Li, if you stick with that original plan and make Wu Li act out the part of an unmitigated jerk, you're going to be short-circuiting your own creative process. Because Wu Li and Jia are sisters with a long history between them, your story can—*must*—be transformed.

For instance: Jia "knows" that Wu Li will never listen to her, because in all their lives together Wu Li has deliberately rejected everything Jia asked her to do. So instead of reporting her findings to Wu Li, Jia can only think to stop the biobomb by sabotaging the project. When Jia is caught, she triumphantly tells her sister that the scabs are now safe; whereupon her sister makes it clear that if she had only known the scabs were sentient, she would have halted the project immediately. In fact, Wu Li was already concerned that the scabs had not been adequately studied before the previous team leader had made the decision to develop a biobomb against them. If Jia had only talked to her, they could have worked together to meet the colony's need to save their crops without wiping out the scabs.

Now, though, Jia has gone off on her own and sabotaged the project, and despite her excellent motives, there's no way she can be trusted again. Her career is over—if Wu Li reports her. Jia, still rejoicing at the fact that Wu Li believes her about the scabs' sentience, assumes that Wu Li will smooth over the whole incident and they can work together from now on. But Wu Li, weeping bitterly, refuses—she is not going to sacrifice her own integrity, even to protect her sister. The incident will be reported accurately; Jia's career is over.

This sets you up for a powerful scene in which Jia, angry and bitter at what she sees as her sister's disloyalty to her, nevertheless goes out into the desert with Wu Li and shows her everything that she's discovered, including introducing her to the one scab with whom she has established a kind of communication. She's doing it for the scabs' sake, she tells herself—but the readers understand that it is really a kind of reconciliation with her sister. Jia now realizes that she *can* trust Wu Li implicitly, that

Wu Li's integrity is so great that she can be trusted to treat the scabs properly.

Perhaps you'll write the story so that Jia knows that the blame is her own, that if only she had trusted her sister before, her own career would not be over. Or perhaps you'll leave her blind to her own failings, so that even as she tells Wu Li all she knows, Jia hates her and will never forgive her. This is perhaps the most painful ending, because your readers will be torn, wishing Wu Li had been more merciful to her sister, but also understanding that Jia is wrong and the ultimate fault is with her.

But you must notice that the most powerful aspects of this story were not in your original idea. In that version the team leader was a cliché villain, the bureaucrat who won't listen to a new idea. In that version, the sabotage of the project was the end of the story. What good would all your world creation do if now you stick with that original story plan? Your reader would probably feel quite dissatisfied at the end; the alert ones would be wondering why you bothered to make the team leader her sister, since it made no difference in the plot.

You have to be willing to change *anything* during the creation phase; only that way can you make the story be true to yourself. There's nothing sacred about your original idea—it was just a starting point. The final story may end up being completely different. In fact, in the story we've been talking about, you may even discover that Jia isn't really the main character anymore. It's Wu Li who has the most painful decision to make—whether to report her sister's sabotage and ruin her career, or save her sister but perhaps endanger other projects because of her sister's proven instability. So instead of telling the story from Jia's point of view, as you always planned, now you realize you must tell it from Wu Li's viewpoint.

The story is nothing like what you first thought it would be. But so what? It's *better*—richer, deeper, truer—than that original idea. The idea did its work: It got you thinking. After that, if you feel bound to stick to it no matter what, that idea becomes a ball and chain that you drag with you through the whole process. Stick with it and you'll get nowhere. Cut it loose and you can fly

So whether you think you already know your story or have no idea what should happen in your newly created world, you can still benefit from going through the following steps in working up the structure of your tale.

1. Whose Story Is This?

When you're deciding whom the story is about, remember that the "hero," the main character, and viewpoint character *don't* all have to be the same person.

Most of us use the term *hero* as an informal synonym for "main character." But in our day we often have an anti-hero as our main character (or protagonist), and it's useful to keep a distinction in mind.

The *hero* is the character that the audience hopes will achieve his goals and desires—the character we're rooting for. There's a moral judgment involved here. We not only care what happens to him, we also *want him to win*.

But the hero isn't always the main character. Sometimes the most important character in a story, the one who makes everything happen, the one whose choices and struggles the story is *about*, is a slimeball, and we watch him in horrified fascination, hoping *somebody* will stop this guy. Sometimes we even sympathize with him, pitying him or even admiring some aspects of his character—but we still don't want him to achieve his goal.

The best example of this is M. J. Engh's masterpiece, *Arslan*, in which the title character is a conqueror whose atrocities at the beginning are only matched by his nihilistic plan for the world he now rules. He is a combination of Hitler and Genghis Khan. We want him to lose; yet we also understand and care about him, are fascinated by him, sometimes in awe of him. By the end of this novel—which I believe is one of the great works of literature in our time—we understand something about one of the great mysteries of modern life: why people loved and followed Hitler, Stalin, Mao, and others whose cruelty seemed boundless. In no way is Arslan the "hero," but he is definitely the main character of the book.

Yet at the beginning of the book you don't necessarily realize this, because the story is told from the point of view of the principal of the local high school. We are seeing events through his eyes as he witnesses Arslan's initial atrocities and then comes to know the conqueror as his enemy. The relationship between the principal and Arslan is very important throughout the story, and we have great sympathy toward the principal, but when, a third of the way through the book, the viewpoint shifts to another character, we are ready. The principal was our eyes and ears, and for a time he was the hero—the person we hoped would win—but he was never the person that the story was about.

By no means is it a rule, but it's often a good idea, when your main character is an anti-hero, to have secondary characters who can function as the focus of your readers' sympathy—in other words, heroes. They don't have to occupy center stage, but they often provide a clarifying moral center. However, if the point of your story is that there *are* no heroes, then this advice doesn't apply—assemble your cast of rakes and racketeers, sleazebags and slimeballs, wimps and wastrels, losers and liars, and have at it.

The Main Character

In choosing the main character for your story, there are a couple of questions you need to consider:

Who hurts the most? In the world you have invented, who suffers the most? Chances are that it is among the characters who are in pain that you will find your main character, partly because your readers' sympathy will be drawn toward a suffering character, and partly because a character in pain is a character who wants things to change. He's likely to *act*. Of course, a character who suffers a lot and then dies won't be a productive main character unless your story is about his life after death. But your eye should be drawn toward pain. Stories about contented people are miserably dull.

Who has the power and freedom to act? Your eye should also be drawn toward movement. Characters who are powerless aren't likely to be doing anything terribly interesting. Your main character usually needs to be somebody active, somebody who can change things in the world, even if it's a struggle.

Remember that you look for people with both the power *and* the freedom to act. Too often—particularly in medieval fantasy—writers think their story must be about rulers. Kings and queens, dukes and duchesses—they can be extravagantly powerful, yes, but too often they aren't free at all. If you understand the workings of power in human societies, you'll know that the greatest freedom to act in unpredictable ways is usually found away from the centers of power.

Let me give you an example: the television and movie series *Star Trek*.

The original series creator wanted characters with the power to make decisions, and centered on the captain and executive officer of a military starship. Unfortunately, however, as anyone who knows anything about the military will tell you, the commanders of ships and armies don't have many interesting adventures. They're almost always at headquarters, making the big decisions and sending out the orders to the people who do the physically dangerous work.

In other words, the lives of commanders (and kings) are generally above the most interesting action. The really neat stuff is going to be happening to the people on the cutting edge—frontline troops, scouts, the people who get beamed down to the planet's surface to find out what's going on. It would be insane for the commander of a ship or any of the highest officers to leave their posts and do common reconnaissance. In any real starfleet there would be teams of trained explorers, diplomats, and scientists ready to venture forth at the commander's orders. If *Star Trek* had been about one such team, the stories would have been inherently more plausible—and there would have been room for tension between the ship's officers and the exploration teams, a rich vein of story possibilities that was virtually untapped.

Instead, *Star Trek* centered around the characters with the highest prestige who, in a realistic world, would have the least freedom. But since commanding officers who behaved like commanding officers would make for boring television, the writers simply allowed these characters to go exploring, constantly leaving their duties on the starship as they merrily went about getting kidnapped, lost, beaten up, or whatever the plot of the week required. Any captain of a ship or commander of an army who behaved like Captain Kirk would be stripped of command for life. But the series would not have worked otherwise.

At this point you might be saying to yourself, "I should be so lucky as to make mistakes like *Star Trek*—I could use a few bestsellers." But the point I'm making is that *Star Trek* could not possibly have succeeded if the captain had actually behaved like a captain. Centering the series around a commanding officer was such a bad mistake that the show immediately corrected for the error by never, for one moment, having Kirk *behave* like a captain.

While a television show can get away with having a captain who acts like the leader of an exploratory team, the readers of prose science fiction have no tolerance for such nonsense. If your hero needs to act like a landing team leader or an industrial spy or a frontline grunt, then you'd better not make him an admiral or a general or a corporate CEO.

Novice writers continue to make this same mistake, choosing as the main character people who don't—or shouldn't—have enough freedom to be interesting. If the story is about a great war, they assume their hero must be the commanding general or the king, when in fact the story might be most powerfully told if the main character is a sergeant or a common soldier—someone who is making choices and then carrying out those choices *himself*. Or the main character might even be a civilian, whose life is transformed as the great events flow over and around him. Think of the movie *Shenandoah*, and then imagine what the story might have been if Jimmy Stewart had played the commander of an army corps. A character who is a loner or who leads a small group—a squad of soldiers, a single family—has so much more freedom to act than people in high office that it's far easier to tell stories about them.

Sometimes the main character *must* be the commander, of course. But don't just assume that to be the case. In fact, a good rule of thumb is to start with the assumption that your story is *not* about the king or president, the admiral or general, the CEO or the hospital administrator. Only move to the characters in the positions of highest authority when you are forced to because the story can't be told any other way. And then be very sure that you understand how people in such positions make their decisions, how power actually works.

Think of the movie *Dirty Harry*. Whatever you may think of the moral message of the film, the author was aware of the fact that real policemen don't go around blowing people's brains out week after week. Yet that was precisely the cliché on television and in the movies in those days—cops who were, in essence, quick-draw gunfighters transposed from the dusty streets of Dodge City to the asphalt of New York or L.A. So the writer played with that cliché—he created a character who, precisely because he acted like a western sheriff, was always in trouble with his superiors.

Furthermore, just like the cliché cops on TV, his partners were constantly getting shot—but in *Dirty Harry* people actually noticed this and considered an assignment as Harry's partner to be a virtual death sentence. They *blamed* him and he actually had to live with the consequences of his decisions. Whatever else the filmmakers might have done wrong, they certainly did that one thing right: They knew something about how a police department works and took that into account in developing their main character. Or at least they did it better than most other cop stories of that time.

Who is your story about? A person who has a strong reason to want the situation to change—and has both the power and freedom to set about trying to change it.

The Protagonist

Who do we hope succeeds? Usually you'll want your audience's sympathy to be with your main character, if only because it's a lot harder for a writer to make an anti-hero work well in a story. But sometimes you can't get away from the fact that wherever the action is, the story must follow. If all the important and interesting choices are being made by the bad guy—especially if the climax depends on what the bad guy does—chances are he's the main character of your story whether you like it or not.

Take the third *Star Wars* movie, *Return of the Jedi*. The first two movies had focused on Luke Skywalker, Princess Leia, and Han Solo—but it was clear that the story was *about* Luke Skywalker. As the movies became hits and penetrated American culture, however, a curious thing was happening. An extraordinary number of children seemed to admire the monstrous villain, Darth Vader. Why did they want to act out the part of this casual murderer?

I suspect it's because, no matter how busy the good guys were, everything they did was in reaction to Darth Vader. *He* was the one calling the shots. He was the one with the power and freedom to act—and, too, he was made somewhat sympathetic by the fact that his body had been ruined and he depended on a machine for survival.

Darth Vader was also the most mysterious—how did he become the way he is? Why did he turn to the dark side of the force? How did he become so powerful? This sense of mystery and awe is one of the things you must look for when searching for the main character of your story. The audience is drawn to the strange, the powerful, the inexplicable.

By the third movie, probably without any of the filmmakers' being aware of it, Darth Vader was the main character, even though Luke, Leia, and Han remained protagonists. Yes, they have neat adventures and discover things about each other (Don't kiss me, Luke: you're my long-lost brother), but all of these events are just devices to get them ready for their confrontation with the one character whose choices actually matter: Darth Vader. It's no accident that the climax of *Return of the Jedi* is Darth

Vader's choice to turn against the evil emperor and save the life of his son — his choice to reject the dark side of the force. Everything came down to Darth Vader's choice. He was the center of the film. It was *his* story. And yet we never, not once, hoped that he would win.

The Viewpoint Character

Often — perhaps I should say *usually* — your main character will also be your viewpoint character. Since I've written a book that is in large measure about what a viewpoint character is (*Character and Viewpoint*), I'm not going to say much more here than this: The viewpoint character is the person through whose eyes we see the action. If it's a first-person narrative, then the viewpoint character is the person telling the tale. If it's a third-person narrative, then the viewpoint character is the person that we follow most closely, seeing not only what he does, but also why; seeing not only what he sees, but knowing how he interprets it, what he thinks about it.

A quick example, from Octavia Butler's novel *Wild Seed* (Warner/Popular Library/Questar, 1980/1988, pp. 138-39):

> *"Anyanwu would say you have on your leopard face now," Isaac commented.*
>
> *Doro shrugged. He knew what Anyanwu would say, and that she meant it when she compared him to one kind of animal or another. Once she had said such things out of fear or anger. Now she said them out of grim hatred. She had made herself the nearest thing he had to an enemy. She obeyed. She was civil. But she could hold a grudge as no one Doro had ever known.*

The viewpoint character at this moment is Doro, and so we are shown not only what was said, but also what Doro thinks of it, how he interprets it.

The passage tells of a conversation between Isaac and Doro, but it is largely *about* a character who is not present, Anyanwu. Obviously, though, she is very important to the viewpoint character, Doro. In fact, she is the protagonist of the story, the person whose side we are on, the person that we hope will win. Doro, on the other hand, is like Arslan and Darth Vader, in that his choices are the cause of almost everything that happens in the story — and his choices are often dark and terrible, so that we hope the good characters can overcome him. He is the main character, an anti-hero whom we only gradually come to understand.

Wild Seed is thus about the struggle between the main character, Doro, and the protagonist, Anyanwu. And Butler quite properly alternates between the two of them as her viewpoint character. There are chapters from Anyanwu's point of view, so that we can see how she interprets events, what she wants, and why; and there are chapters from Doro's point of view, so we can also see the world the way he sees it and get some idea of his purposes. The story could probably be told from just one of these viewpoints — but it would be much harder for us to understand and sympathize with the character whose viewpoint we never saw.

The viewpoint character will always be important to the audience, if only because the audience has come to understand that character better than anyone else. Usually this means you'll want your main character to be the viewpoint character, just as you'll usually want your main character to be the protagonist.

But there are times when you simply can't do this. In mysteries, for instance, where the point of the story is to discover who committed the murder, it is traditional to make the viewpoint character the detective's sidekick. Why? Because the detective usually knows the identity of the murderer a good while before the end of the book. If he were the viewpoint character — if we were inside his head — the suspense would bleed away far too soon. So Nero Wolfe's stories are told by Archie Goodwin and Sherlock Holmes's by Dr. Watson.

There's another strategy, however, and that is to make the detective *not* be the main character of the novel. This is the strategy Ross MacDonald and other "hard-boiled detective" authors use. The detective is the viewpoint character — we see everything through his eyes — but the story's focus is on the characters caught up in the events surrounding the murder. Theirs are the lives in turmoil; they are the people in pain. While the detective often gets emotionally involved, he is not the person whose life needs to be resolved. And the suspense now is moved, at least in part, away from the question of whodunnit and toward the question of how these people are going to reestablish their lives. Thus we can find out a bit earlier in the story who the murderer was — and still be eager to read on and discover the whole outcome.

Yet even when the viewpoint character is not the main character of a novel, he is nevertheless a major character, if only because we get to know him so well. So he has to be well developed, and his personal dilemmas must also be resolved by the end of the story or the audience will, quite properly, feel cheated.

Who should your viewpoint character be? If it isn't the main character or the protagonist, your viewpoint character must be someone in a position to see — and usually take part in — the major events of the story. If you find that your viewpoint character is constantly finding out about the most important events as people tell him about it after the fact, you can be almost certain you have chosen the wrong viewpoint character.

Here are some guidelines for choosing a viewpoint character who isn't the main character:

1. The viewpoint character must be present at the main events.
2. The viewpoint character must be actively involved in those events, not always a chance witness.
3. The viewpoint character must have a personal stake in the outcome, even though the outcome depends on the main character's choices.

(Of course, like all rules, these can be broken. You can have a viewpoint character who is *never* there for the main events — if your story is at least partly about the fact that he is frustrated because he constantly misses the important moments. But this moves your story toward comedy, which is fine if comedy is what you're writing; and it focuses your story on the viewpoint character's absence and not the events themselves. Break the rules if you like — but make sure you understand the consequences and know how to turn them to your story's advantage.)

2. Where Does the Story Begin and End?

Once again we must distinguish between some terms that are often used interchangeably.

The *myth* of the story, as opposed to the *text*, consists of what happens and why. The myth is usually very simple, but it also begins long before the beginning and goes on long after the end. This is because causal chains are infinite. For instance, the story of Oedipus is usually thought to begin when his parents, to save themselves from the prophecy that their son will kill his father and marry his mother, bind his ankles and abandon him to die.

But the causal chain actually begins long before. The parents did what they did because they lived in a culture that believed in prophecy and in which it was not thought to be a heinous crime to leave a monstrous child to die. And there are reasons why their society adopted these beliefs and attitudes, and reasons for those reasons. The causal chain also continues long after — as we know from the plays *Oedipus at Colonus* and *Antigone*, which are about the consequences of the events and choices made in the play *Oedipus Rex*.

So the myth of the story is actually a long network of cause and effect that begins long before the story and continues long afterward. You, however, must choose a point where the story begins and a point where it ends. You must decide the story's structure.

The Beginning That Sets Up the End

Let's go back to Octavia Butler's *Wild Seed*. The story is about Doro, a character born thousands of years ago. He is immortal, not because his body cannot die, but because whenever his body is about to die — or at other times — his spirit or essence immediately and involuntarily jumps to the nearest living person, taking over their body completely. Thus the displaced spirit ceases to exist, while Doro lives on in his victim's former body.

Butler could have begun *Wild Seed* with the scene of Doro's first transition from one body to another — the time when he first realized that he could not die. It is indeed a powerful scene, because the first person he killed, the first person whose body he took, was his own mother. Not understanding what happened, he looked down and saw his old body — his own body, lying there dead in "his" arms — and panicked. How had he suddenly become a woman? He screamed; his father, trying to calm and comfort the person he thought was his wife, touched him and Doro inadvertently jumped to *his* body. Without meaning to, Doro discovered his powers by killing his own parents. It took a long time before he came to terms with what he was and what he had done. Those events could have been a novel in their own right.

In fact, that's one reason why Butler was correct not to begin *Wild Seed* with that event. She does include an account of his first killing — but it comes on page 177 of a 179-page book. It is a flashback, a memory. Receiving that memory makes the audience revise its view of Doro, so that we reinterpret all that he has done from the beginning. Yet by coming when it does, that event doesn't take over the book. It is one more piece fitted into the whole.

If it had come at the beginning, the event is so strong, so powerful, that the audience would have expected the whole story to be about Doro's struggle to know and control himself. It would have made Anyanwu a fairly minor character, late-come and perhaps a bit contrived. "Oh, right," we would say. "Doro is a slimeball until the love of a good woman transforms him. How convenient that she happens along."

Butler wanted to tell the story of Doro's relationship with Anyanwu, a woman with extraordinary talents of her own—a shapechanger, a healer. Butler's story ends when Anyanwu and Doro reach a sort of accommodation with each other—when Doro is at last able to love and respect another human being instead of regarding them all as his tools and subjects, when Anyanwu is at last able to reconcile herself to a world that includes a monster like Doro—and reconcile herself to the fact that she understands and, in a way, loves him despite his monstrousness. The only way Butler could do that was to make Doro and Anyanwu equal in our eyes—and if we spent the first fifty pages of the novel watching Doro struggle with his powers several thousand years before Anyanwu is born, that balance between them would be almost impossible to achieve.

All that I've said, however, comes with hindsight. Perhaps Butler was aware of all this; perhaps she wasn't. I haven't asked her. What matters is that there *is* a way to determine where a story should begin and end.

Since the story will end with their accommodation with each other, the story must begin in such a way that the audience will expect that ending. That is, the beginning must make the audience ask questions that are answered by the story's ending, so that when they reach that ending, they recognize that the story is over.

The beginning of a story creates tension in the audience, makes them feel a *need*. The ending of that story comes when that tension is eased, when that need is satisfied. So in determining your structure, it is essential for you to make sure your beginning creates the need that your ending will satisfy; or that your ending satisfies the need that your beginning created!

You'd be amazed how many stories fail precisely because the writer began one story and ended another. Or began the story long after it should have begun, or long before. Yet how can you know where your story should begin, or what the right ending is? Most writers learn to do this instinctively—or never do it at all. But there is a way to look at your own story, discover the possible structures, and choose among them.

The MICE Quotient

All stories contain four elements that can determine structure: Milieu, Idea, Character, and Event. While each is present in every story, there is generally one that dominates the others.

Which one dominates? The one that the author cares about most. This is why the process of discovering the structure of a story is usually a process of self-discovery. Which aspect of the story matters most to you? That is the aspect that will give you your story's structure.

Let's take each element in turn and look at the structure that would be required if that is the dominant element in the story.

The Milieu Story. The milieu is the world—the planet, the society, the weather, the family, all the elements that came up during the world creation phase. Every story has a milieu, but in some stories the milieu is the thing the storyteller cares about most. For instance, in *Gulliver's Travels*, Swift cared little about whether we came to care about Gulliver as a character. The whole point of the story was for the audience to see all the strange lands where Gulliver traveled and then compare the societies he found there with the society of England in Swift's own day—and the societies of all the tale's readers, in all times and places.

So it would have been absurd to begin by spending a lot of time on Gulliver's childhood and upbringing. The real story began the moment Gulliver got to the first of the book's strange lands, and it ended when he came home.

Milieu stories always follow that structure. An observer who will see things as we would see them gets to the strange place, sees all the things that are interesting, is transformed by what he sees, and then comes back a new man. Stephen Boyett's *Architect of Sleep* follows that structure, as a modern man passes through a cave in Florida and comes out in a world in which it is the raccoon and not the ape that gave rise to a sentient species. He is the only human in a world of brainy raccoons.

But it isn't only in science fiction and fantasy that this structure occurs. James Clavell's *Shogun*, for instance, follows exactly the same structure. It begins when his European hero is stranded in medieval Japan and ends when he leaves. He was transformed by his experiences in Japan, but he does not stay—he returns to "our" world. Other stories are told along the way—the story of the shogun, for instance—but however much we care about those events, the closure we expect at the end of the story is the main character's departure from Japan.

Likewise, *The Wizard of Oz* doesn't end when Dorothy kills the Wicked Witch of the West. It ends when Dorothy leaves Oz and goes home to Kansas.

As you work with your story, if you realize that what you care about most is having a stranger explore and discover the world you've created, chances are that you'll want to follow the Milieu Story structure. Then your beginning point is obvious—when the stranger arrives—and the ending is just as plain—the story doesn't end until he leaves (or, in a variant, he finally decides not to leave, ending the question of going home).

And who is your viewpoint character? The stranger, of course. The milieu is seen through his eyes, since he will be surprised by and interested in the same strange and marvelous (and terrible) things that surprise and interest the audience.

The Idea Story. "Ideas" in this sense are the new bits of information that are discovered in the process of the story by characters who did not previously know that information. Idea stories are *about* the process of finding out that information. The structure here is very simple: The Idea Story begins by raising a question; it ends when the question is answered.

Most mystery stories follow this structure. The story begins when a murder takes place; the question we ask is, Who did it and why? The story ends when the identity and motive of the killer are revealed.

In the field of speculative fiction, a similar structure is quite common. The story begins with a question: Why did this beautiful ancient civilization on a faraway planet come to an end? Why are all these people gone, when they were once so wise and their achievements were so great? The answer, in Arthur C. Clarke's "The Star," is that their sun went nova, making life impossible in their star system. And, ironically, it was the explosion of their star that the wise men saw as the sign of the birth of Christ. The story is told from the point of view of a Christian who, like most of the audience at the time Clarke wrote the story, will believe that this must have been a deliberate act of God, to destroy a beautiful civilization for the sake of giving a sign to a few magi.

Many other stories follow this pattern. A question is raised:

Who buried this monolith on the moon, and why did it give off a powerful radio signal when we uncovered it?

Why did this young man try to kill himself after his brother was drowned in a storm while they were boating together, and why is he so hostile to everyone now?

The story may take many twists and turns along the way, but it ends when the question is finally answered:

In *2001: A Space Odyssey*, we find out that the monolith was left for us to find, so that when we reached it the master race that created it would know we were ready to move on to the next stage in our evolution.

In *Ordinary People*, we find out that the main character tried to kill himself because he believes that his mother blames him for not dying in his brother's place; and he discovers that he has been lashing out at everyone around him because he can't express his anger at his brother for letting go of the hull of the boat—for dying.

When the mystery is resolved, whether by a detective, a scientist, or a psychiatrist, the main tension is resolved and the story is over. So Idea Stories begin as close to the point where the question is first raised and end as soon as possible after the question is answered.

You may notice that some mysteries don't reach the discovery of the body until many pages into the story. Aren't they following the Idea Story structure? In most cases they are, but they can bend the rule about starting with the question because the mystery tradition is now so well established that mystery readers take it for granted that someone will be killed; they're willing to wait a little while to find out who dies. Thus mystery writers have the freedom to spend quite a few pages establishing the character of the detective or setting up the society in which the murder will take place. But the audience is quite aware that a murder *will* take place, and soon becomes impatient if the writer takes too long getting to it.

Outside the mystery genre, there is a good deal less leeway because the audience doesn't know that the story will be about the process of answering a question. If you begin the story by establishing character at great length, and don't come to the main question until many pages into the tale, readers will expect the story to be about the character, and not about the question; if you then end the story where the mystery is solved but never resolve the character, they'll be quite frustrated. You must begin the story you intend to end—unless you *know* that the audience already knows what the story is about.

The Character Story. All stories have characters, and in one sense stories are almost always "about" one or more characters. In most stories, though, the tale is not about the character's character; that is, the story is not about who the character is.

The Character Story is a story about the transformation of a character's role in the communities that matter most to him. The Indiana Jones movies are event stories, not character stories. The story is always about what Indiana Jones *does*, but never who he *is*. Jones has many problems and adventures, but at the end of the movie his role in society is exactly what it was before — part-time archaeology professor and full-time knight-errant.

By contrast, Carson McCullers's *Member of the Wedding* is about a young girl's longing to change her role in the only community she knows — her household, her family. She determines that she wants to belong to her brother and his new wife; "they are the we of me," she decides. In the effort to become part of their new marriage she is thwarted — but in the process her role in the family and in the world at large *is* transformed, and at the end of the story she is not who she was. *Member of the Wedding* is a character story; the Indiana Jones movies are not.

It is a common misconception that all good stories must have full characterization. This is not quite true. All good Character Stories *must* have full characterization, because that's what they're about; and other kinds of stories *can* have full characterization, as long as the reader is not misled into expecting a Character Story when that is not what is going to be delivered. On the other hand, many excellent Milieu, Idea, and Event Stories spend very little effort on characterization beyond what is necessary to keep the story moving. The Indiana Jones stories don't require us to get more of Jones than his charm and his courage. In short, he is what he does in the story, and while it's delightful to meet his father and learn something of his background in *Indiana Jones and the Last Crusade*, the first two movies certainly did not leave us wishing for more characterization. That's not what they were about.

Having said that, I must also point out that to be taken seriously as a writer, and not just a writer of speculative fiction, you must be able to draw interesting and believable characters; and most stories are improved when the author is skillful at characterization. But only when the story is *about* the transformation of a character's role in his community do you have a true Character Story.

The structure of a Character Story is as simple as any of the others.

The story begins at the moment when the main character becomes so unhappy, impatient, or angry in his present role that he begins the process of change; and it ends when the character either settles into a new role (happily or not) or gives up the struggle and remains in the old role (happily or not).

Just as mystery readers give authors a little leeway at the beginning to establish the detective and the situation out of which the murder arises, so also the readers of character stories will accept the narrative equivalent of an "establishing shot." After all, if we are to care whether the character succeeds in changing, we must understand what it is he's changing *from*.

But, with rare exceptions, you should still begin the story as close to the point at which the character begins to attempt to change as possible. Few things in fiction are more tedious than reading a Character Story that begins many years — and many pages — before the character actually attempts to change his life. The author may be doing a lovely job of showing us the character's past and letting us in on his thoughts and feelings, but we keep waiting for something to happen, asking, "Why am I reading this? *So what?*"

This is not because we want adventure — no car chase is required. All we need is a sense of direction, a sense that the character is in motion. I have read many a student story in which it's not until page ten — or twenty, or fifty — that we finally get a sentence like this: "That was the day when Albie decided he had had enough." By then it's too late — the attempt to change will usually seem too feeble for the long build-up that preceded it.

The character's attempt to change doesn't have to be a conscious decision; it can be an inadvertent move, an instinctive seizing of opportunity. The character can find himself wondering, "What did I do *that* for?" — or thinking, "Why didn't I do that *long* ago!"

Characters in the other kinds of story *can* change, too, though they don't have to. You can embed Character Stories as subplots within Milieu, Event, and Idea stories, but in that case the characters' changes are not the climax of the whole work, not the signal to the reader that the story is over, that the tension of the tale is now released.

Even within a Character Story, the main character is not the only one who will change. Since a person's role in a community is defined by and defines his relationships with other people, a change in his own role will change theirs, too. Much of the plot in a Character Story rises out of the other characters' resistance to change. Often the climax will involve the final battle between characters in their war to establish incompatible identities. Think of *The Barretts of Wimpole Street*, in which Elizabeth Barrett's love for Robert Browning makes her become so dissatisfied with her role in her father's family that she decides to leave. But her father is unwilling to allow any such change in any of his children — it would require *him* to go through more self-redefinition than he is willing to bear. The story ends when Elizabeth cuts loose and leaves; we see that she has successfully transformed herself, and we also relish the forced transformation in her tyrannical father's life.

The Barretts of Wimpole Street absolutely follows the structure of a character story: No matter how many characters are in flux, the Character Story begins close to the point where the main character begins to attempt to change his role, and ends at the point where the struggle ends.

If the transformation of character is what you care about most in the story you want to tell, then identify which character's changes trigger all the other transformations. That's your main character, and your story begins when he just can't take it anymore.

The Event Story. In the Event Story, something is wrong in the fabric of the universe; the world is out of order. In the ancient tradition of Romance (as opposed to the modern publishing category), this can include the appearance of a monster (*Beowulf*), the "unnatural" murder of a king by his brother (*Hamlet*) or a guest by his host (*Macbeth*), the breaking of an oath (*Havelok the Dane*), the conquest of a Christian land by the infidel (*King Horn*), the birth of a child of portent who some believe ought not to have been born (*Dune*), or the reappearance of a powerful ancient adversary who was thought to be dead (*Lord of the Rings*). In all cases, a previous order — a "golden age" — has been disrupted and the world is in flux, a dangerous place.

The Event Story ends at the point where a new order is established, or, more rarely, where the old order is restored, or, rarest of all, where the world descends into chaos as the forces of order are destroyed. The story begins, not at the point where the world becomes disordered, but rather at the point where the character whose actions are most crucial to establishing the new order becomes involved in the struggle. *Hamlet* doesn't begin with the murder of Hamlet's father; it begins much later, when the ghost appears to Hamlet and involves him in the struggle to remove the usurper and reestablish the proper order of the kingdom.

Macbeth is eccentric in that the main character is the source of the disorder rather than its opponent. Yet it doesn't begin with the murder of the king, either; it begins much *earlier*, when the witches first put the improper thought of becoming king into Macbeth's mind. And it ends when, after much struggle to reconcile himself with the chaos he brought into the world, Macbeth is killed, thus restoring a proper order.

Because the story concerns the restoration of the proper order of the universe, it's not surprising that Romance traditionally concerns itself with grand people—royalty, nobility, heroes, even demigods. But this is not necessary. Think of Megan Lindholm's superb fantasy *The Wizard of the Pigeons*; the hero is a wizard, yes, but he is also a Seattle streetperson living on garbage and the occasional handout. Lindholm draws the real Seattle street life very convincingly; yet her hero is no less concerned with the fact that an enemy has crept into his modest, orderly little "kingdom," sowing confusion and threatening destruction.

And the disorder in the world can be even more subtle, the character even less obviously heroic. Jane Austen's *Emma* concerns a woman who acted on bad advice and refused to marry the man who would have brought her happiness. This private decision is nevertheless a violation of the natural order of the universe in which Emma lives; she herself becomes then a disorderly force, sowing difficulties in the lives of others until at last she realizes she made a mistake and marries the man she should have married in the first place. The story begins at the point where Emma becomes involved in the disorder and ends where order is restored.

Almost all fantasy and much—perhaps most—science fiction uses the Event Story structure. Nowhere is it better handled than in Tolkien's great trilogy. *Lord of the Rings* begins when Frodo discovers that the ring Bilbo gave him is the key to the overthrow of Sauron, the great adversary of the world's order; it ends, not with the destruction of Sauron, but with the complete reestablishment of the new order—which includes the departure of Frodo and all other magical people from Middle Earth.

Notice that Tolkien does not begin with a prologue recounting all the history of Middle Earth up to the point where Gandalf tells Frodo what the ring is. He begins, instead, by establishing Frodo's domestic situation and then thrusting world events on him, explaining no more of the world situation than Frodo needs to know right at the beginning. We only learn of the rest of the foregoing events bit by bit, as the information is revealed to Frodo.

In other words, the viewpoint character, not the narrator, is our guide into the world situation. We start with the small part of the world that he knows and understands and see only as much of the disorder of the universe as he can see. It takes many days — and many pages — before Frodo stands before the council of Elrond, the whole situation having been explained to him, and says, "I will take the ring, though I do not know the way." By the time a lengthy explanation is given, we have already seen much of the disorder of the universe for ourselves — the Black Riders, the hoodlums in Bree, the barrow wights — and have met the true king, Aragorn, in his disguise as Strider. In other words, by the time we are given the full explanation of the world, we already care about the people involved in saving it.

Too many writers of Event Stories, especially epic fantasies, don't learn this lesson from Tolkien. Instead, they imagine that their poor reader won't be able to understand what's going on if they don't begin with a prologue showing the "world situation." Alas, these prologues *always* fail. Because we aren't emotionally involved with any characters, because we don't yet *care*, the prologues are meaningless. They are also usually confusing, as a half-dozen names are thrown at us all at once. I have learned, as a book reviewer, that it's usually best to skip the prologue entirely and begin with the story — as the author should also have done. I have never — not once — found that by skipping the prologue I missed some information I needed to have in order to read the story; and when I *have* read the prologue first, I have never — not once — found it interesting, helpful, or even understandable.

In other words, writers of Event Stories, *don't write prologues*. Homer didn't need to summarize the whole Trojan War for us; he began the *Iliad* with the particular, the private wrath of Achilles. Learn from Homer — and Tolkien, and all the other writers who have handled the Event Story well. Begin small, and only gradually expand our vision to include the whole world. If you don't let us know and care about the hero first, we won't be around for the saving of the world. There's plenty of time for us to learn the big picture.

Deciding which is which. How do you know which structure your story should follow? The fact is that most stories could be made to follow any of these structures. The most important thing is that you must end the story that you begin. If you promise a Character Story by the way you begin your tale, then your story can only achieve closure by having the main character end his attempt to change his role—not by solving a mystery! And if you promise an Idea Story by beginning with a vital question, you can't achieve closure by having a character find a new role in life.

Still, there is almost always a best structure for a particular story. You often can't find it until you've attempted a draft and find yourself bogged down only a few pages or chapters into it (often a pretty good sign that you're using the wrong structure, beginning at the wrong place). Chances are, that early exploratory draft will end up being thrown away—but not too soon! First, read it carefully, not to fix up the prose or correct minor story flaws, but rather to discover what you like best in it.

What did you spend the most time on? Were you fascinated with the main character's unhappy relationships with other people? Then you may need to structure it as a Character Story. Did you devote a lot of time to exploring the world, showing its wonders and oddities? Then perhaps you need to structure it as a Milieu Story, bringing in an outsider as the viewpoint character. Or is it the grand events, the disorder in the world that interests you? In that case, you need to identify who it is that will end up restoring good order to the world and begin with his or her first involvement in the struggle against disorder.

One thing, though, that you must beware of, and that is the natural tendency of novice writers to automatically structure all their stories as Idea Stories. Judging from student and workshop stories over the years, both in and out of the field of speculative fiction, I believe that most stories that fail do so because the writer, having thought up a neat idea for a story, then structured the story so that it leads up to the moment when that neat story idea is revealed.

This is fine, of course, when the story really is about the struggle of a character to find the answer to a question. But it's terrible when it's the readers, not the characters, who are doing the struggling. The mystery in these cases is not a single question—Who killed this man? Why does this large planet have such low gravity? Instead the questions are more basic. What's going on? Why am I reading this?

A student story I read recently consisted of a long monologue by a man giving someone directions to a small town, but as he spoke, he constantly digressed, telling of memories associated with certain landmarks along the way. Only near the very end did we discover that this monologue was a telephone conversation; that the man knew the person he was speaking to; and that they planned to meet. And the most important information of all was only implied in one of the last sentences: The person he was speaking to was his lover, coming for a rendezvous in his old hometown.

That sort of sudden surprise ending (Ah! *That's* what it all meant!) rarely works, and for this reason: Because the writer had to labor so hard to conceal what was actually going on in the story, he was unable to accomplish anything *except* concealment. The entire story consisted of withholding from the reader every speck of information that would have made the story interesting. If he had begun by telling us that the man was giving directions to his lover, then he could have used that monologue to show us their relationship and how the man's life led up to betraying his wife with this other woman; he could have shown us the pain and guilt — not to mention the ecstatic anticipation of the tryst.

In other words, it could have been a Character Story, in which the man was struggling to change his role and, at the end, either succeeded or failed; it could have been an Event Story, in which either his marriage or his love affair was a bit of disorder in the universe which had to be resolved; it could even have been a Milieu Story, in which he took his lover exploring through the back-country world he grew up in. But by structuring it as a mystery, he left himself none of these possibilities. Indeed, he couldn't even write honestly. Because the author couldn't tell us that the man was talking to his lover, it was impossible to have the man even speak as men speak to their lovers — the monologue was as impersonal as if he were giving directions to strangers in a passing car. There could be no reference to shared memories between them; no expressions of emotion that might give things away.

So as you look at your bogged-down first draft, look to see how much of your effort is spent on withholding information, and then examine whether your reader has any reason to care about what's going on as long as that information is withheld. Most novice writers imagine that this is how suspense is created — by holding back key information from the reader. But that is not so. Suspense comes from having almost *all* the information — enough information that the audience is emotionally involved and cares very much about that tiny bit of information left unrevealed.

Usually the only information that you withhold is this: what is going to happen next. The climax of a story isn't created by suddenly discovering what's going on. The climax of the story is created by suddenly resolving issues that have been causing the audience a great deal of tension throughout the story. There's no tension without information.

If you find that all your stories are structured as Idea Stories in which the reader never knows what's going on until the end, then stop it. Forbid yourself to use that structure again until you have mastered one of the others. You *only* use the Idea Story structure when the *characters* are searching for the answers to questions. When the characters all know the answers and only the audience is asking the questions, you are definitely using the wrong structure. Your story idea may be terrific — but your execution of the story is killing it.

What about plot — deciding which scenes to show, structuring those scenes, building from one minor climax to another? I told you from the first that I would concentrate on those aspects of writing that are peculiar to speculative fiction. Plotting is handled no differently in sf than in any other genre. If you feel you need help in that area, I recommend Ansen Dibell's book *Plot*, a companion volume in the same series as my own *Character and Viewpoint*.

Most of the things we've talked about so far — world creation, structure — I usually work on extensively before ever writing a draft of a story or novel. There are many other writers — perhaps more — who can only develop these aspects of a story while writing narrative drafts, and that's fine, too. In fact, I continue creating my world and revising and clarifying my story's structure while writing drafts, so I know that much of the best invention only comes while you're actually telling the tale. Your order of working is entirely up to you — as long as you actually do all the work I've talked about in these chapters.

The unfortunate thing is that too many writers — though not very many writers actually making a career out of this — skip the entire process of invention and construction. Once they have the first glimmer of an idea they proceed immediately to writing a draft and spend all their effort on producing beautiful prose. Alas, they're wasting their time. As William Goldman had a character say in *Boys and Girls Together*, speaking of a play that was in rehearsal, "Wash garbage, it's still garbage." It doesn't matter how beautifully a story is performed if the story itself — what happens and why — is crippled with cliché or badly structured.

Still, after all your preparatory work, there comes a time when you have to produce the draft that counts. The world is well invented, the structure is solid. Now you have to get this story from your mind into the minds of your readers. And that's where your skill with stories must be matched by skill with communication. You've got to have the language; you've got to be able to *write*.

4. Writing Well

Good writing is good writing, no matter which genre you work in. But there are some areas of special concern to writers of speculative fiction. Don't be misled by the fact that this is the shortest section of the book. It is brief because the basic information is simple; but the technique itself is difficult and requires practice—particularly the handling of exposition—and you'll get the best results from the chapter if you reread it more than once, using the techniques shown here to analyze your own story drafts.

1. Exposition

One area in which sf differs from all other genres is the handling of *exposition*—the orderly revelation of necessary information to the reader.

It may seem that in the last chapter I told you two bits of conflicting advice. First I warned you against using prologues with Event Stories and said you should only reveal information about the disorder in the world as it becomes available to the viewpoint character. Then I told you *not* to withhold information, but instead to let the readers know at least as much as the characters do about what's going on.

It's not a contradiction—but it *is* a balancing act. It's like watering a plant. Too little water and it dries up and dies; too much water and it rots and drowns. Information is to your audience as water is to a plant—it's the life of the story, and yet you have to keep it in balance. Too much raw information up front and the reader can't keep it all straight; too little information and the reader can't figure out what's happening. The result in either case is confusion, impatience, boredom. The audience quickly learns that you don't know how to tell a story, and you've lost them.

Instead, information must be trickled into a story, always just enough to know what's happening. If the audience must know a fact in order to understand what's going on, then you must either present the information at that moment, or make sure that the information was available—and memorable—earlier in the text. In particular, if the viewpoint character knows a fact that gives a different meaning to an event, then the audience must also know that fact—though if the viewpoint character *doesn't* know, it's perfectly all right for the audience to share his ignorance.

This balance is especially difficult to achieve in science fiction and fantasy, because our stories take place in worlds that differ from the known world. We not only have to introduce characters and immediate situations, we also have to let readers know how the rules of our universe differ from the normal rules, and show them the strangeness of the place in which the events occur.

In the early days of science fiction, when the genre was still being invented, key information was given in huge lumps, often by having one character explain things to another. This was often badly handled, as when one character explained things to another who already knew it:

"As you know, Dr. Smith, the rebolitic manciplator causes the electrons of any given group of atoms to reverse their charge and become anti-electrons."

"Yes, Dr. Whitley, and of course that will cause an immediate explosion unless the rebolitic manciplation is conducted inside an extremely powerful Boodley field."

"And the only facility in Nova Scotia that is capable of maintaining a Boodley field of sufficient power is—"

"That's right. Dr. Malifax's lab on his houseboat in the Bay of Fundy."

I hardly need to tell you that this is no longer regarded as a viable solution to the problem of exposition.

Exposition is even more complicated today because of the development of an extremely tight third-person-limited point of view, in which the only information given is what the viewpoint character sees and thinks, with no obvious intrusions on the part of the narrator. Most professional fiction today uses this viewpoint because of its great advantages. But the disadvantage is that you generally can't "notice" anything that the viewpoint character doesn't notice, or "think of" anything that the viewpoint character doesn't think of.

This is particularly challenging for speculative fiction writers. If your viewpoint character is a participant in the strange society you're trying to reveal to your audience, he wouldn't suddenly start noticing things he's taken for granted all his life.

So you have to reveal information very carefully, and usually by implication. The best way to tell you what I mean is to show you, by going through the opening paragraphs of Octavia Butler's novel *Wild Seed*. (I've chosen this book because nobody handles exposition better than Butler—and also because it's a terrific novel that you ought to read for the sheer pleasure of it.)

Let's start with the first sentence:

> *Doro discovered the woman by accident when he went to see what was left of one of his seed villages.*

You have just been given an astonishing amount of information—but it has been done in such a way that you probably aren't aware of how much you already know.

Naming. First, we know the name of the viewpoint character: Doro. Later we'll learn that Doro has many names, but Butler gives us the name by which he thinks of himself—and whenever we're in Doro's viewpoint that's the only name used for him. Bad writers keep changing the name of their viewpoint character, thinking they're helping us by telling us more information: "The starship captain walked onto the bridge. Bob glanced over and saw the lights were blinking. 'What're you thinking of, Dilworth?' said the tall blond man." Is Bob the starship captain? Or is Bob Dilworth? And is it Bob or the starship captain who is the tall blond man? One tag per character, please, at least until we know them better. Above all, don't coyly begin with pronouns for the viewpoint character and make us wonder who "he" or "she" is—give us a name *first*, so we have a hook on which to hang all the information we learn about that character.

Second, we know that Doro will discover "the woman," and we assume that this discovery will be important to the story. Because Butler is a first-rate writer, that assumption is correct—she would never mislead us by putting a trivial character so portentously in the opening sentence. Yet she doesn't name the woman yet. In part this is because naming two characters immediately is often confusing. Too many names at once are hard to keep track of, and we aren't always sure which is the viewpoint character. Another reason for not naming "the woman," however, is because at this exact moment in the story—as Doro goes to see what is left of a village—he doesn't know her name. The narrator knows her name, of course, but at this moment Doro does not, and so it's right not to give that information to the reader.

Abeyance. What else do we learn from these three sentences? Doro didn't intend to meet the woman. His purpose at the time was to see what was left of—what? A "seed village."

What in the world is a seed village?

We don't know what a seed village is. And Butler doesn't tell us—because Doro, who knows perfectly well what a seed village is, wouldn't stop and think about that information right now. But in due time we *will* find out what a seed village is. So we hold that question in abeyance. We have a hook with the label "seed village" over it; we trust that the author will let us know in due course what information should be hung on that hook.

This principle of abeyance is one of the protocols of reading speculative fiction that makes it difficult for some people who aren't familiar with the genre to grasp what's going on. Experienced sf readers recognize that they don't know what a seed village is, and that the author doesn't expect them to know. Instead, this is one of the differences, one of the things that is strange in this created world, and the author will in due course explain what the term means.

But the reader who is inexperienced in sf thinks that the author expects him to already know what a seed village is. He stops cold, trying to guess what the term means from its context. But he *can't* guess, because there isn't enough context yet. Instead of holding the information in abeyance like a small mystery, he is just as likely to think that either the writer is so clumsy that she doesn't know how to communicate well, or that this novel is so esoteric that its readers are expected to know uncommon terms that aren't even in the dictionary.

This is one of the real boundaries between sf and non-sf writing. Science fiction and fantasy writers handle exposition this way, by dropping in occasional terms as the viewpoint character thinks of them, and explaining them only later. The sf reader doesn't expect to receive a complete picture of the world all at once. Rather he builds up his own picture bit by bit from clues within the text.

Implication. Butler is not being obscure; she is being *clear*. While "seed villages" goes unexplained, we *are* told that this is merely one of them, and that Doro thinks of more than one seed village as "his." Furthermore, "seed village" is not a wholly obscure term. We know what a village is; we know what *seed* means when it's used as an adjective. Seed potatoes, for instance, are small potatoes or parts of potatoes that are planted in the ground to grow into larger ones. By implication, Doro is somehow using villages as seed — or perhaps he has the villagers growing seeds for him. We aren't sure, but we do know that Doro is working on growing *something* and that he has more than one village involved in it.

This, again, is one of the protocols of reading sf. The reader is expected to extrapolate, to find the implied information contained in new words. The classic example is Robert Heinlein's phrase "The door dilated." No explanation of the technology; the character doesn't think, "Good heavens! A dilating door!" Instead, the reader is told not only that doors in this place dilate, irising open in all directions at once, but also that the character takes this fact for granted. The implication is that many — perhaps all — doors in this place dilate, and that they have been doing it for long enough that nobody pays attention to it anymore.

The sf writer is thus able to imply far more information than he actually states; the sf reader *will* pick up most or all of these implications. Indeed, this is one reason why you must be so rigorous about creating your worlds to quite a deep level of detail, because your readers will constantly be leaping past what you actually say to find the implications of what you're saying — and if you haven't thought things through to that level, they'll catch you being sloppy or silly or just plain wrong.

Literalism. The protocols of abeyance and implication, which give you a great deal of power, also remove one of the tools that mainstream writers rely on most heavily: metaphor. Especially at the beginning of a speculative story, all strange statements are taken *literally*. "Seed village" isn't a metaphor, it's what this village actually *is*.

I think of a story by Tom Maddox that appeared some years ago in *Omni*. In the first or second paragraph he had passengers taken from their airplane to the terminal on what he called a "reptile bus." I was teaching an sf literature course at the time, and my students were pretty evenly divided between those who had been reading sf for years and those who had never read it before that semester.

The majority of the experienced sf readers reported the same experience

I had: At least for a moment, and often for quite a way into the story, we thought that Maddox wanted us to think that reptiles were somehow being used for airport transportation. We pictured a triceratops with a howdah, perhaps, or an allosaur towing a rickshaw. It was an absurd sort of technology, and it would have strained credulity—but many sf stories use such bizarre ideas and make them work. Maddox might have been establishing a world in which bio-engineers had created many new species of very useful but stupid dinosaurs.

Those who had never read sf, however, were untroubled by such distractions. They knew at once that "reptile bus" was a metaphor—that it was a regular gas-burning bus with several sections so it snaked across the tarmac in a reptile-like way.

This is one of the key differences between the sf audience and any other. When confronted with a strange juxtaposition of familiar words, both groups say, "What does the author mean by this?" But the sf audience expects the term to be literal, to have a real extension within the world of the story, while the mainstream audience expects the term to be metaphorical, to express an attitude toward or give a new understanding of something that is part of the known world.

When an sf writer says, "She took heavy mechanical steps toward the door," there is always the possibility that in fact her legs are machinery; the mainstream writer assumes this metaphorically expresses the manner of her walking, and would regard that word usage as a grotesque joke if she *did* have artificial legs.

This doesn't mean that you, as an sf writer, are forbidden to use metaphor. It *does* mean that early in a story, when the rules of your created world are not yet fully explained, you have to avoid metaphors that might be confusing to experienced sf readers. Later, when the rules are firmly set, your readers will know that terms that imply things that are not possible in your world should be taken metaphorically.

Do recall the difference between metaphor, simile, and analogy. Similes and analogies, which explicitly state that one thing is *like* another thing, are still available; it's only metaphors, which state that one thing *is* another thing, that are forbidden. "You could treat Howard Merkle like dirt and he'd still come fawning back to you, just like a whipped dog," a simile, is perfectly clear and usable in speculative fiction, whereas the metaphor "Howard Merkle was a dog, always eager to please no matter how you treated him" is problematical early in a speculative fiction story, because it *could* be taken literally.

Also, beware of analogies that remove the reader from the milieu of the story and remind him of the present time. "The aliens had facial structures like eyebrows, only arched in an exaggerated way, so they walked around looking like a McDonald's advertisement." This sentence would be fine in a near-future story about contact with aliens; McDonald's would presumably still be around. But the same sentence would be quite out of place if the story were set in a time and place so different from our own that the characters do *not* have McDonald's restaurants as part of their daily experience. In that case, such a sentence is clearly the writer talking to the contemporary American reader, not the narrator creating the experience of another time and place. And it's almost worse if you try to compensate for this dislocation by making it explicit: "The aliens' eyebrows arched like the logo of that ancient fast-food restaurant, McDonald's, which Pyotr had seen once in a history book about the twentieth century on Earth." This sort of thing throws the reader right out of the story. There's a natural impulse to compare something strange to something that will be familiar to the reader—but as a general rule you should use only similes and analogies that would also be available to the characters in the story, so that the entire experience of reading contributes to the illusion of being in the story's milieu.

Piquing our interest. All this, and we're only one sentence into *Wild Seed!* Remember, though, that while it takes pages to explicate all the processes going on here, the sentence takes only a moment to read; most of these processes are quite unconscious, and while Butler certainly chose this sentence carefully, many of the things that are right about it are simply good habits that she instinctively follows—like immediately naming the viewpoint character and *not* naming a character whose name is unknown to the viewpoint character.

But you can also be certain that she thought carefully before choosing the term "seed village," to make sure that it was evocative and interesting. It is the mysteriousness of that term that first piques our interest, that makes us wonder, "Who is Doro? What is it he's trying to grow? In what sense is this village *his?*" Without that term, all we're left with is the much less intriguing mystery of who "the woman" is.

Mystery? Is *Wild Seed* an Idea Story? Not at all. These "mysteries" are very small, and no time at all is spent on them. Doro isn't wondering who the woman is or what a seed village is. He hasn't met this woman yet, so we know that when he does meet her, our questions will be answered; and he already knows what a seed village is, so we fully expect that we will soon be informed as well. These are transient mysteries, part of the exposition process, not the kind of story-driving mystery that can give shape to an entire novel.

It's important, especially at the beginning, that you reveal information that promises your reader an interesting story to come. Those promises must be honest ones that you intend to keep. Because Doro is set up as the kind of character who can somehow "own" villages, we see him as a bit larger than life—Butler definitely will deliver on this promise. And the concept of seed villages is absolutely central to the story; it isn't a trivial bit of strangeness to be tossed in and thrown away. In other words, Butler isn't just giving us random but interesting information to fool us into going on—she's giving us interesting information that is vital to the story.

A workshop in exposition. Let's go on now with the entire opening paragraph of *Wild Seed*:

> *Doro discovered the woman by accident when he went to see what was left of one of his seed villages. The village was a comfortable mud-walled place surrounded by grasslands and scattered trees. But Doro realized even before he reached it that its people were gone. Slavers had been to it before him. With their guns and their greed, they had undone in a few hours the work of a thousand years. Those villagers they had not herded away, they had slaughtered. Doro found human bones, hair, bits of desiccated flesh missed by scavengers. He stood over a very small skeleton—the bones of a child—and wondered where the survivors had been taken. Which country or New World colony? How far would he have to travel to find the remnants of what had been a healthy, vigorous people?*

What do we learn in this paragraph? First, the immediate situation is absolutely clear—we aren't wondering what's happening. Doro has come to one of his seed villages and finds all the people gone—either dead or taken off into slavery—and he now is thinking about going to find the survivors.

The immediate situation is powerful. The image of the bones and hair and bits of flesh, the small skeleton of a murdered child — these arouse a sense of loss and outrage in us, even when we hear about such things happening to strangers. There are good guys and bad guys already being sorted out in our minds: The slavers are bad and the villagers are their innocent victims.

But this is still only part of what Butler is telling us in this paragraph. Many other things are hinted, things that we may not consciously pick up but which are nevertheless working on us unconsciously; they are the foundation on which we'll build the rest of the story and the rest of the world of this book.

For instance, we are getting a sense of the time frame of the story. The village is mud-walled, which suggests a pre-technological society — but the slavers have guns, a key piece of information that tells us that if the story takes place on Earth, it is set in fairly recent times. By the end of the paragraph, Butler's reference to New World colonies gives us the strong implication that the story is set on Earth during the era when there was a market for slaves in the New World; and that means that this village is almost certainly in Africa. ("New World" might also be taken literally, as another planet, but the feel of the story so far is low-tech, and so a space-faring culture is not our first assumption.) All these inferences are confirmed by later information, so that readers who don't get all this from the first are not abandoned — but the fact remains that Butler has essentially set the time and place for us within the first paragraph and *without* stopping the action to tell us outright that we are in Africa in the slave-trading era.

Even more important is the information we're given about Doro. The fact that he regards a mud-walled village as "comfortable" tells us that he doesn't feel at all out of place in primitive settings and that he can feel at home in one of "his" villages.

Doro also knew that the people were gone *before* he reached the village. How did he know it? He might have observed that there was no one working in the fields; he might have noticed it because there was none of the usual noise of the village. Butler doesn't tell us how he knows, though, so the possibility remains open that his knowledge is not based on the normal means of ascertaining such things. The reader may or may not notice it, but the implication is there.

We get Doro's attitude toward the slavers — he thinks of them as greedy—but then as Doro observes the village, as we are shown the bones and hair and bits of flesh, the child's skeleton, what surprises us is his lack of appropriate emotion. Standing over the skeleton, he doesn't wonder *who* the child was, doesn't grieve at all, doesn't even think with outrage of the inhumanity of the butcherous slavers. Instead he wonders where and how far the survivors have been taken. And his wondering is not sympathetic ("He imagined their terror as they were dragged away from the screams of their dying loved ones . . ."), but wholly practical: "How far would he have to travel?" Even his memory of the people is the way a man remembers a valued but unloved animal: "A healthy, vigorous people." The phrase "his seed villages" begins to be clarified: Doro is the farmer, and the human beings themselves are his crop.

The next two paragraphs tell us that Doro is not unemotional—but confirms that his relationship with other people is indeed strange:

> *Finally, he stumbled away from the ruins bitterly angry, not knowing or caring where he went. It was a matter of pride with him that he protected his own. Not the individuals, perhaps, but the groups. They gave him their loyalty, their obedience, and he protected them.*
> *He had failed.*

It's his pride that is injured; he hates failing. His affections are not for individuals, but rather for groups. It was the village as a whole that he cared for, not the people. He really is just like a farmer, who would hardly notice the death of a few stalks of wheat but would be bitterly angry at the destruction of an entire field.

Yet in the strength of his emotions, he does stumble away, not knowing or caring where he goes. So while he doesn't relate to other people in a natural way and clearly regards them as being less than he, like a flock or a field, he *is* still human himself, after a fashion. It is possible to understand at least some of his feelings. He is at once strange and familiar.

It is in the fourth paragraph that we are given the final bit of information about Doro that tells us exactly how strange he is:

> *He wandered southwest toward the forest, leaving as he had arrived—alone, unarmed, without supplies, accepting the savanna and later the forest as easily as he accepted any terrain. He was killed several times—by disease, by animals, by hostile people. This was a harsh land.*

Yet he continued to move southwest, unthinkingly veering away from the section of the coast where his ship awaited him. After a while, he realized it was no longer his anger at the loss of his seed village that drove him. It was something new — an impulse, a feeling, a kind of mental undertow pulling at him. He could have resisted it easily, but he did not. He felt there was something for him farther on, a little farther, just ahead. He trusted such feelings.

Notice how casually Butler lays in the information that he is killed more than once. She doesn't make a big deal about it, because to Doro being killed isn't terribly important. But to us it is, and the very fact that Doro can be killed several times and still continue to move southwest tells us that he is very strange indeed. He looks down on human beings like crops or herds because he is, somehow, immortal, able to be killed and yet go on.

We know now that he owns a ship and that its crew expects to meet him at a prearranged place — this suggests what we will eventually discover is a network of servants and possessions that reaches all around the world.

We also know that he is sensitive to sources of information that normal people just don't have — he is drawn by a "mental undertow" and willingly goes along with it because he trusts such feelings. Obviously, he's had experiences like this before.

And because Butler is one of the best writers of sf during a time when there are many very good ones, this whole passage is imbued with emotions and we are carried along by language that flows and swirls with grace and power.

Two paragraphs later, after a line space (on a manuscript, you mark such spaces with an asterisk), she changes point of view. Now we're seeing what's going on through the eyes and mind of a woman named Anyanwu. Naturally, if we remember the reference to "the woman" in the first sentence, we assume that Anyanwu *is* that woman — and we are correct. A good writer like Butler would never confuse us by leading us to incorrect assumptions.

We soon realize that Anyanwu is, in her own way, as strange and remarkable as Doro. First, we know that she is capable of killing — she once killed seven men who were stalking her with machetes — but that she regrets it and regards killing as a terrible thing to be avoided when possible.

She is aware of a lone intruder now, prowling the underbrush near her.

We immediately assume—again correctly—that this is Doro, though of course Butler can't say so because Anyanwu doesn't know him yet. Anyanwu is still "the woman" to Doro; Doro is still "the intruder" to Anyanwu.

We also learn that Anyanwu is a healer, and that "often she needed no medicines, but she kept that to herself"—so she, too, has some kind of transcendent power. Like Doro, she thinks of the people of her village as "her" people—but they are not just one village among many, and she doesn't just come to pay a visit now and then. She lives among them; she serves them by healing them and also by allowing them to spread stories about her healing powers, so they can profit when people from other villages come to her to be healed.

A reference to Anyanwu's long life and her "various youths" implies that she, like Doro, is somehow immortal—but, unlike Doro, she fears death and tries to avoid it through vigilance. So they do not have the same powers and don't live by the same rules. Doro can be killed by men or animals or disease and yet go on living; Anyanwu lives a long time but must avoid murderers in order to do it. Anyanwu fears no poison because of her superior understanding of them, not because she can't die.

And yet all this information is conveyed within a tense scene in which Anyanwu is mentally tracking the intruder—Doro—and trying to determine whether she is going to have to kill him in order to defend herself.

At this point we are only three pages into Butler's novel, yet she has conveyed an enormous amount of information to us, all through the thoughts and actions of her two viewpoint characters. We have never, not for a moment, been aware of the exposition, because she never stopped the action to tell us.

Furthermore, she has not yet explained the whole situation; we don't yet know that the disorder in the world is Doro himself, a man who can't die, who has to kill whether he wants to or not. True to the Event Story structure, Butler has begun the story exactly where her protagonist, the person who will restore order to the world, gets involved in the struggle to solve the problem—the point where she meets Doro. The actual meeting is on the fourth page of the book; she is aware of him by the middle of the second page; and Butler refers to that meeting in the very first sentence of *Wild Seed*.

From the very beginning, Butler promises us the story she means to tell, and then delivers on every promise. From the start we know why we should read on, and as we read we effortlessly receive every bit of information we need to have in order to understand the whole story. Many writers handle sf exposition very well; almost all handle it with at least minimal competence. No one does it better than Butler; I urge you to pick up any of her books or stories. Read them once for pleasure; then study them to learn how it's done.

2. Language

Some stories demand different kinds of writing; what's good for one story may not be good for another.

Diction. In her essay "From Elfland to Poughkeepsie," Ursula K. LeGuin makes such a point with great eloquence: When fantasists are writing about people of high station living in heroic times, a more formal, elevated level of diction is called for. On the other hand, when you're creating low comedy, diction can range from the mock heroic to the coarse.

However, there is great danger in trying for elevated diction—primarily because it's so easy to overdo it or do it very badly. You have to read a lot of brilliantly written formal prose before you're able to handle it well—and there isn't much of it being written these days. LeGuin herself and Gene Wolfe are the two most reliable sources of that level of diction within the field of speculative fiction; outside it, you are best served by reading Jane Austen or, for a contemporary example, Judith Martin; when writing as "Miss Manners" she uses excellent formal diction, often with devastating irony.

Here is the same scene, three ways.

Sevora read the letter, showing no emotion as she did. Tyvell only realized something was wrong when the letter slipped from her fingers and she took a single hesitant step toward him. He caught her before she could fall to the floor.

He laid her gently on the thick fur before the hearth, then sent his dwarf to fetch the surgeon. Before help arrived, however, her eyes opened.

"The surgeon is coming," Tyvell said, gently holding her hand.

"Read the letter," she whispered. "Lebbech has destroyed me."

★ ★ ★

Sevora perused the missive, displaying none of the turmoil of her feelings on her impassive, stonelike face. Tyvell only became aware of the tumult within her when she let fall the curled parchment and staggered toward him. With the utmost hurry he caught her in his arms before her delicate frame could strike the floor.

Gently he laid her on the pliant bearskin before the merrily dancing flames of the hearth, then sent Crimond, his astonished and frantic dwarf, to fetch the cirurgeon. Before the diminutive servant's abbreviated stride could bring the desired aid, however, Sevora resumed consciousness and her eyes fluttered open.

"Fear not," said Tyvell, stroking the smooth white skin of her hand. "I have sent for the cirurgeon."

"I need him not," whispered Sevora. "How can I be holpen now by his herberies? Nay, even his knife shall not serve me in my present need. Under the hideous spells of Lebbech I now lie destroyed."

★ ★ ★

Sevora read the letter as best she could, moving her lips and stumbling now and then when there were too many letters in a word. Tyvell realized it was bad news when Sevora crumpled it up and stumbled toward him, her eyes rolling back in her head. Here he was minding his own business and now she had to fall on him in one of her damn faints.

He dragged her over by the fireplace and yelled for Crimond to go get the doctor because Sevora was out cold. The dwarf took off like a shot, but before he could get the old surgeon sobered up enough to come, Sevora had gotten tired of Tyvell patting her hand. She opened her eyes and glared at him.

"Look, I already sent for the doctor," he said. She always got so ticked off at him when he didn't take her faints seriously.

But it was the letter she was thinking about—it really was pretty bad. "Screw the doctor," she said. "Lebbech's got me cursed six ways from Tuesday. If we can't get these spells off me before the baby's born, I'm toast."

The first example is plainly meant to be taken seriously as a tale of highborn people caught up in heroic events. The second example, however, is trying too hard. There is no grace in a surfeit of adjectives, and high language doesn't consist of using twisted "poetic" syntax and needless archaisms like "holpen" and "cirurgeon." Indeed, elegance usually requires simplicity and clarity.

The third example is plainly meant to be comedy — but I have read many a story that was in dead earnest that was scarcely less funny in the choice of words. Modern slang is just as obnoxious in serious formal language as phony archaism; few solemn fantasists would use expressions like "I'm toast" or "six ways from Tuesday," but even more normal diction like the use of the terms *look* or *pretty bad* or even *bad news* — these would all be out of place in the first example.

If your characters are elevated, their language should be also; if they are common, then common language is appropriate. Furthermore, the language of the narrative should be a good match for the language in the dialogue; it was quite annoying, for instance, in a fantasy I read recently, set in Elizabethan England, to have the lowborn characters speak like highborn heroic Shakespearean characters — while the narrative was in fairly common modern English. The constant shifting only called attention to the language and distracted from the story.

If you want to see the levels of language clearly differentiated within a single work, the best teacher (as is so often the case) is Shakespeare. Look carefully at plays like *A Midsummer Night's Dream* and *The Taming of the Shrew*. In both there are "high" characters and "low" characters. The high characters speak in blank verse, with clean, elegant, figured diction. The low characters speak in unrhymed lines, with coarse humor and often with mangled English. Yet there is hilarious comedy in both levels of diction — and both levels of diction are extremely well written. Formal English isn't "good" while colloquial English is "bad" — good diction is the diction that is most appropriate to the scene at hand.

Profanity and vulgarity. There are no hard-and-fast rules of decorum anymore. You can pretty much use the language that you want, though the magazines do have *some* limits. That doesn't mean that writers are "free" now, however. It only means that the burden of deciding what to do is thrown back on the writer.

What you must remember is that language has real effects on people. If you have a character who constantly uses foul language, that language will have an effect on the people around him. But if you actually put that language explicitly in your story, that bad language will have a similar effect on your audience. They will learn the fact that your character is a foul-mouthed boor, which is what you intend; but a substantial number of them will also be put off by your story to exactly the degree they would have been offended by the character, which may not be at all what you have in mind.

I would never change anything essential in order to pander to a particular audience segment, but it would be just as absurd to include something nonessential when it would drive away an audience segment that might otherwise enjoy the story. It always comes down to what is or is not essential. Freedom of the press means that the decision is entirely up to you; it doesn't mean that you always have to decide in favor of being offensive.

However, if you decide against using vulgar or profane language, I urge you simply to leave out expletives entirely rather than replacing them with euphemisms. One well-known writer tried using the acronym *tanj* (there ain't no justice) exactly as the coarse Anglo-Saxon word for copulation is used. "Tanj off!" "Get your tanjin' hands off me!" It may have been a noble experiment, but as far as I could tell it proved that euphemisms are often worse than the crudities they replace, because they make both the story and the character seem pretty silly. Either use indecorous language or don't use it—don't try to simulate it, because, unless you have more genius than I've ever heard of, it just won't work.

On the other hand, when you're creating an alien society, one of the best ways to suggest their values and culture is through your choice of which words are regarded as too indecorous to be used by decent people. In our culture, the words associated with coitus and elimination are too powerful to be spoken without care—and this tells you something about us. What about a culture in which the words for *eating* are regarded as indecent, while the words we are shocked by are easily used? A visitor from contemporary America might get into a lot of trouble moving through a culture where sex is as casual as blowing your nose, but where the idea of *owning* something, of keeping property that you withhold from general use, is as outrageous as pederasty. He's going to get his face slapped and not have the faintest idea why.

5. The Life and Business of Writing

Your story is finished. Now it's time to . . .

No, I'm getting ahead of myself; I know too many writers who never feel their stories are finished.

Oh, the story has an *ending*, say these writers. But it's not ready to send off yet. Or: I want to do one more draft, clean up a few rough edges. Or: My workshop gave me some great ideas for revision, but I can't get to it for a while—I'll wait to send it off till I have a chance to get those taken care of. Or: The story just isn't good enough to publish yet.

I've heard all the excuses, but too often they're pure rationalization. It might be true enough that the story isn't ready for publication—but that isn't why you aren't sending it out. No, you're hanging on to this manuscript for one reason only.

Raw, naked fear.

Fear that you'll send it out and it will come back and then you will have *positive proof* that you're no good and you shouldn't be a writer and then your whole identity will come crashing down around your ears—so, as long as you can hold off sending out the story, you can continue to believe that this story *might* be published instead of knowing for sure that it won't.

Of course, as long as you delay you also have no chance of knowing for sure that it *could* be published.

When your story is finished, let it go do its work. Don't wait for it to gather dust on your shelf. Sure, if you let it sit there for a year and pull it down and look at it again, you'll find all kinds of dumb mistakes that you'd *never* make today because you're so much better now. But then, if you had sent it out and it had been purchased by a magazine, it would be appearing in print right now, and while you would still find those flaws in it, at least you would have been paid for it and your story would be in print and—here's the good part—your readers will like the story just fine the way it is.

Am I advocating that you send out second-rate work? Am I saying that readers are fools who can't tell good work from bad?

Not at all. I'm saying that you should send out, today, the best work you are capable of doing today. Of course you'll do better a year from now. But a year from now you should be writing the story that you care about and believe in at that time—not reworking *this* year's story.

And your readers *can* tell good work from bad, quite easily. In fact, they can do a better job of it than you can. Because the more you fiddle with your story, rewriting this paragraph or that one, the more likely you are to make it *worse*. There are things you instinctively do when the story is in its first rush out of your head that are truer and better than anything you'll come up with as you second-guess, revise, intellectualize.

Of course you'll edit before you send it out—you want to have the cleanest, clearest, most professional manuscript you can. But at some point— soon—you need to stop and say, "That's today's story. I'll mail this day's story to this day's editors. Then I'll begin to think about the next story— the one I'll write tomorrow."

You grow a whole lot more as a writer by getting old stories out of the house and letting new ones come in and live with you until they grow up and are ready to go. Don't let the old ones stay there and grow fat and cranky and eat all the food out of the refrigerator. You have dozens of generations of stories inside you, but the only way to make room for the new ones is to write the old ones and mail them off.

1. Short Fiction

The market for short speculative fiction is limited—but within those limitations, it's just about the healthiest short fiction market in America. No other paying market is so open to new writers; no other short story market offers so much notice, such an excellent entry into a real career.

The short story market consists of magazines and anthologies. The magazines and their editors were discussed in the first chapter. Remember that the shorter your story is, the better its chance of getting published; but also remember that no other fiction market is so receptive to the novelette length (7,500 to 15,000 words). However, editors are grateful whenever they get a short story (fewer than 7,500 words), because it's easier to fit into a magazine issue — and the shorter the stories, the more different titles that can fit into the same number of pages. But they'll *buy* a longer work, and from a newcomer, too, if it's strong. Novellas, however (more than 15,000 words), are usually not possible for a newcomer. If a magazine editor is going to tie up that many pages with one story, the author had better have a name that will sell copies when it's printed on the cover.

The anthologies are books — usually paperbacks — that consist of short stories by many different authors. Quite a few are reprint anthologies, which include only stories that previously appeared somewhere else. Also, many anthologies are by invitation only; you can't just send a story to the editor. And most original anthologies (books that include never-before-published stories) don't continue month to month or year to year the way magazines do, so that by the time a new writer hears about one, the book is already full.

So your best bet, with several exceptions, is to try your short story with the magazines first. Here are the exceptions:

Writers of the Future. At this writing, the Writers of the Future contest continues in good health. I'm very skeptical of most writing contests, but this one, run by Bridge Publications, is the real thing. Their prize money is high — $4,000 for the annual winner, $1,000 for the quarterly winners, and lesser prizes for second and third place. They also pay you separately for publication in the *Writers of the Future* anthology (edited by Algis Budrys) — and their payment rate is better than any of the magazines except *Omni*. The anthology sells very well, and you might even earn royalties from it besides the upfront payment.

Each year's winners of the Writers of the Future contest have been offered a completely free writing workshop taught by professional writers (I have taught at a couple); Bridge Publications even pays for their transportation, housing, and meals. Bridge also does an extraordinarily good job of helping you get media attention. Best of all, because the contest winners are announced quarterly, your story is tied up no longer than it takes most of the magazines to respond to a regular submission.

The Writers of the Future contest has helped launch the careers of many fine writers. The competition is tough, but it's worth sending your best work there first. (To find the address and rules for submission, check the most recent *Writers of the Future* anthology in your bookstore or library; complete contest information is always included.)

Other anthologies. There are always at least a few other original anthologies looking for new writers. Andre Norton and Marion Zimmer Bradley both edit ongoing series that are particularly open to fantasies and women writers. Pulphouse Publishing, based in Oregon, publishes a "hardcover magazine"—an original anthology in a lovely hardcover edition. To find out the current addresses and rules for submission, look for their anthologies in the science fiction/fantasy section of your local bookstore, or check the genre magazines—like *Locus*.

Locus. Other anthologies may crop up from time to time—I even have plans in the works to edit an original anthology series myself. Anthologies that are truly open to everyone almost invariably announce that fact in a magazine called *Locus*. *Locus* is to the speculative fiction field what the *Wall Street Journal* is to finance and *Variety* is to show business—not everybody loves it, but everybody reads it.

Locus publishes listings of almost every speculative fiction book published in America and the United Kingdom; it also reviews many books, publishes a monthly genre bestseller list, and conducts an annual award poll. Published and edited by Charles N. Brown, it reports on sf and fantasy conventions and sf and fantasy publishing in other countries, interviews major figures in the field, and passes along a bit of gossip—though its standards of truth are high enough that if you enjoy really scurrilous slander you'll have to look elsewhere.

In short, *Locus* is as close as our field comes to a professional journal, and you're crazy if you don't subscribe, at least at the beginning of your career. I don't expect the address to change, so I'll list it here:

Locus Publications
PO Box 13305
Oakland CA 94661

Write for the current subscription rate or for information about foreign subscription agents.

Fanzines. *Locus* began as a fanzine—a privately published amateur magazine. There are dozens, perhaps hundreds of fanzines published all over the world, filled with lively commentary about science fiction and fantasy. Many—perhaps most—are now "mediazines," oriented toward science fiction and fantasy television shows and movies like *Star Trek, Star Wars,* and *Dr. Who*. There are also magazines of criticism, gossip, and more than a few that publish fiction.

In fact, the fanzine community is so complex and interesting that it's impossible to do it justice here. It *is* important, however, that you know that there are fanzine publishers who are quite serious about publishing fiction. Some, like Stuart David Schiff with his horror magazine *Whispers,* cross over the line from amateur to professional publication, taking their regular writers with them.

If you are writing mainline science fiction, then you should not consider publishing in the fanzines — if the professional magazines and anthologies won't publish you, chances are your stories aren't good enough for publication yet. But if your stories are offbeat, experimental, or in genres with less magazine coverage, like horror or heroic fantasy, then fanzines may well represent the *best* market for your short fiction.

How do you know? It's easy. Find the magazines — in the dealer room at a science fiction convention, in the ads in *Locus,* in a science fiction/fantasy specialty bookstore, or by sheer dumb luck. Then read an issue or two, and if you like the stories a lot, the magazine is good enough. If, on the other hand, the stories seem amateurish and embarrassing to you, don't submit there. It's that simple. If you are in the audience for the fiction a magazine publishes, then that's a good audience for you to write for.

Submit to the best market. However, do not submit to fanzines *first* if there's a paying professional market for which your stories might be appropriate. Fanzines get almost *no* attention in the sf field (with the exception of horrorzines, and that's only because Karl Edward Wagner reads them all and selects stories from them for his annual anthology of the year's best horror). The book editors generally don't read the fanzines; fanzine stories are never nominated for major awards; and fanzine publication generally counts for nothing on your résumé.

I've known more than a few writers who published their first five or six stories in fanzines. These were fine stories that could have advanced their careers, but they *never submitted them* to the professional markets. Why? "I didn't think I was good enough yet." They allowed their personal fears (or personal modesty) to keep them from reaching the markets that would have reached the widest audience and advanced their careers.

The writer's self-image. Writers have to simultaneously believe the following two things:

1. The story I am now working on is the greatest work of genius ever written in English.
2. The story I am now working on is worthless drivel.

It's best if you believe both these things simultaneously, so that you can call on Belief 1 when you're deciding whether to mail the story out, Belief 2 when going over the story to revise it, Belief 1 when choosing which market to submit it to, Belief 2 when the story is rejected (of course, I *expected* to get this back), and Belief 1 again when you put it back in an envelope and mail it to the next-best market.

Of course, believing two contradictory facts at the same time is sometimes referred to as madness — but that, too, can be an asset to a writer.

The rule is: Submit to the best market first. But define the word "best" your own way. There's one high-paying market that I never submit to because I think that working with that editor isn't worth the aggravation. There's another publisher that I will always give anything he asks because I trust him and he has been there for me far beyond the letter of the contract. This may be a business, but you're still a human being, and if you ever forget *that* and start to make all your decisions on the basis of money alone, then it doesn't much matter how well you handle the business end of things, because your fiction will soon reflect the decay of your soul.

Foreign markets. There are short fiction markets in other countries. They're hard to hear about, and unless you read the language, it's hard to judge the quality. Two, however, are so excellent that they constitute legitimate markets to which you might wish to submit your best work.

Interzone, published in England with a rather small circulation, has an excellent reputation for publishing powerful, dangerous, daring stories. Not everyone appreciates everything they publish — but issues of *Interzone* are never boring, and some of the finest writers in the field appear there first.

Hayakawa's SF magazine is Japan's only professional-level science fiction magazine. Naturally, any English-language story they receive has to be translated before publication. I urge you *not* to submit to them work that has already been rejected by all the American magazines — their standards are just as high as American standards, and it's far more effort for them to consider English-language submissions. But if you think a story you've written might be particularly well received in Japan, *Hayakawa's SF* magazine is a good choice. Several noted American authors, starting with Bruce Sterling, have had stories published there first; it was no barrier to later U.S. publication.

2. Novels

If you're writing fantasy or horror, you probably have to start with novels — the short fiction market is too small. And even if you're writing science fiction, you can't live on short stories alone; at some time you'll almost certainly switch to novels.

So, now you've finished writing your first novel. What do you do with it?

Queries. There are only a limited number of houses publishing science fiction on a regular basis. The leaders at this writing are Bantam/Doubleday/Dell, St. Martin's/TOR, Berkley/Putnam/Ace, and Ballantine/Del Rey; other major lines include DAW, NAL/Signet, Warner/Popular Library, and Morrow (hardcover only). At the time you're deciding where to send your book, check the bookstore and see if any more need to be added. Look up the addresses of the publishers in *Writer's Market* or *Novel and Short Story Writer's Market*. (You also might want to telephone the publishers to find out the names of their science fiction and fantasy editors, so you can put the right name on the query letter.)

Then prepare a query and send it to all of them at once.

That's right. Don't waste years of your life waiting for the editor at House X to remember that your manuscript is still sitting in the four-ton pile beside his bed waiting to be read. The query consists of the first couple of chapters and a brief outline of the rest of the book, right to the end. The outline is not in "I.A.1.a." form; it's a present-tense recounting of what happens and why. Period. None of the neat information about the world you've created, no snatches of dialogue from the best scenes — just what happens and why.

On top of this you may place a one-page synopsis consisting of no more than three paragraphs. This synopsis consists of the kind of overview that is usually placed on the back cover of a paperback. It does *not* include praise of the author or quotes from reviewers—it simply tells what the book is about in a way that helps the reader decide whether to buy or not. You include this, not because you expect it to end up on the back cover, but rather to hook the editor—and *show* the editor how your book might also hook its audience. Study a lot of back covers before you try writing such a synopsis, and if you still don't understand how it's done, don't include one. It's not mandatory, and it's only helpful if you do it right.

Cover letter. Finally, the first sheet in your query parcel is a letter that, under your name, address, and phone number, says:

Dear [Editor's Name],

Enclosed are the first two chapters and an outline of my fantasy novel <u>Doom of the Dyphnikei</u>. Would you like me to send you the complete manuscript?

Three of my stories have been purchased, two by <u>F&SF</u> and one by Marion Zimmer Bradley for <u>Swords and Sorceresses</u>; they have not yet appeared. You may recall that I spoke to you at BayCon in San Jose last May, and you suggested you'd like me to send you this query.

Sincerely,

[Your name]
encl: Synopsis, chapters 1&2, outline

That's it. That's all. And if you *don't* have any legitimate credentials and/ or *haven't* met the editor, then the entire body of your letter is that first paragraph. Its message is simple and clear: First, that you are querying, not submitting this novel; this is communicated by the fact that you say "Would you like me to send the complete manuscript?" Because you include this sentence, your package is not a multiple submission, which is a no-no, but rather a multiple query, which is a perfectly acceptable—indeed, *necessary*—thing to do. Second, you have identified your book's genre. It is a fantasy novel.

Anything else you say, beyond legitimate credentials that won't otherwise be known to the editor, is superfluous and will probably make you seem amateurish. After all, you're not striking up a friendship, you're establishing the terms under which you're asking the editor to read part of your novel. Once the editor has read your partial and outline and likes it, *then* your relationship can start getting friendly and chatty. Until that time, any attempt at friendship with an editor you don't know well will seem presumptuous at best. Nothing shouts "unprofessional" like an overlong cover letter.

Is it "who you know"? Is it true that making friends with editors is the key to getting published? That it's "who you know," not how well you write?

There *is* a sense in which that's true. Editors are human—when a manuscript by a friend or by a writer whose work they know lands on their desk, they're more likely to give it an early reading, and they may read it with a bit more sympathy, a bit more willingness to forgive flaws.

Furthermore, a known writer who has already built a following is more likely to be a good financial risk than a new writer who has no audience waiting eagerly for the next book. If two manuscripts are of equal interest and quality, the more established writer will usually get the nod.

That only means that to break in, you may have to be better than average, especially if you come in at a time when the market is retrenching rather than expanding. It *doesn't* mean that there's no hope for you unless you get to know an editor.

The truth is that an editor who intends to keep his job doesn't publish books he doesn't believe in, even if they're written by his dearest friends. Editors don't work in a vacuum. Other people in his company read those books. The sales force often *doesn't* read it, but they certainly have to sell it. Any editor who has a habit of buying nags and slipping them in among the thoroughbreds will soon be applying for a position at another company.

Besides, every editor *I've* known wouldn't knowingly do it anyway. They're in this business because they love books—*good* books. And that's what they hope to find every time they look at a manuscript. It's the greatest moment in an editor's life, to start reading a manuscript by a complete unknown and discover, page after page, that this writer knows what she's doing. You ought to talk to them the day after, the week after such a discovery. As a reviewer, I sometimes get letters — maybe once a year, probably less often — in which the editor says, "This is something special. I hope you have a chance to give it a good read." Editors don't do this for their *friends*. They do this for the stories they love best. That could be your story.

That's the only secret to getting ahead — write the kind of story that makes editors and readers respond so powerfully that they can't contain themselves, they have to tell everybody about your work. If you wrote a substandard book, then knowing an editor only gets it rejected sooner, with a nicer letter. If you wrote a good book, then not knowing any editors beforehand may mean it takes longer to get accepted — but the editor who buys it will be all the more excited to have discovered you.

3. Agents

For your short fiction, you don't need an agent.

For your first novel, you don't need an agent until you've got a contract offer from a publisher.

Unless you have a track record with short fiction, the kind of agent who'll take you on before you've actually received an offer from a publisher is usually not the kind of agent who'll be able to do much to advance your career. Once you have that contract in hand, however, you can send it to the agent *you* want to have representing you and say, "House Y has sent me this contract. Would you like to represent me?"

Wait a minute! You already have the contract — why do you need an agent now?

Not so you can get more money — only in very rare cases is an agent going to be able to get you one dime more for a first novel. What you need the agent for is all the other stuff. To get obnoxious clauses removed from the contract before you sign it. To get vital clauses inserted — the reversion of your rights if the publisher lets your book go out of print, for instance.

Subsidiary rights. Above all, you need an agent to make sure you never yield to the publisher any unnecessary subsidiary rights. Don't give away your foreign rights or your broadcast and film rights, ever, unless the publisher pays you a *lot* of additional money for them — and even then I don't advise it. If you retain those rights, a U.S. agent with an agreement with a foreign agent can make sales in other countries that your publisher will *never* make for you. Only a handful of my books have made me more from U.S. sales alone than they have brought in from foreign sales — but almost none of that came from the few publishers, early in my career, to whom I yielded the foreign rights to a book.

True, Dutch rights don't go for much money. But it's $500 more than you would have had if you'd left those rights with your U.S. publisher, because they're not going to be pushing your little old first novel in the Netherlands, they're going to be pushing somebody else's big book. Or, in many cases, they won't have a presence in the Netherlands at all.

As for movie rights, don't expect Hollywood to beat down your door. But now and then somebody'll nibble. They'll option a story or a book. Most options never turn into sales — but in the meantime, you can spend the $3,000 or $5,000 option money. I've never yet had such a check arrive that I couldn't find a use for. I've also never had such a check arrive as a result of anything a publisher did for me.

That's what your agent can do. Hold on to your rights, and then exploit them. Remember, your agent works for *you*. Your publisher doesn't. Who's going to protect your interests better?

Ten percent. There are those who would have you believe that the best agents nowadays are charging their clients fifteen percent. Don't believe it, not for a second. The best agents charge their clients a ten-percent rate for U.S. sales. (Percentages rightfully go up when they have to split the proceeds with a foreign agency.) When an agent charges a higher rate, it's either a confession that he's not good enough to make a living at the ten-percent rate, or an admission that he thinks of himself as being some sort of packager or co-author of your work. He'll brag about the extra services he performs. I promise you, you don't want or need any services beyond the ones my agent provides for me — at ten percent.

How do they persuade writers to accept fifteen percent? If you don't buy that "everybody charges that now" line, then they work on your self-esteem. "I'm sorry, I just can't afford to take on a *marginal* writer at ten percent." They prey on your insecurities.

One hundred percent of the value of your book comes from what you put into it. It's generous of you to give someone else ten percent of the gross income from that book, just for handling the selling and the contract. Don't you forget it. If you can't find an agent for ten percent, then find your own foreign agent directly, get a New York lawyer to work over the contracts for you, read them carefully yourself, and live without an agent. They need you more at ten percent than you need them at fifteen.

Reading fees. Generally you should steer clear of agencies that charge reading fees. I know that reading the slushpile eats up an enormous amount of an agent's time—but you won't be on the slushpile. That's because you won't even seek an agent until you have a contract—and when you have a contract, prospective agents know you're the real thing. There's no risk. You're not slushpile.

Besides, agents are business representatives, not writing schools. Who do you think will respond to your manuscript at that agency that charges a reading fee? As likely as not, some poor would-be agent or would-be writer who's reading the agent's slush for a fee. What does he know?

There may be exceptions. There may be reading-fee agencies that actually give you some value for your money. I don't believe it, but I admit that it's possible. The trouble is, you have no way of knowing which is which until you've spent your money.

It's sad how many new writers waste time and hope trying to get an agent at a point in their careers when an agent won't do them any good— and the kind of agent they're likely to get can do them serious harm.

Believe in yourself. You don't need some magic trick to sell your stories—you just need to do your best work on a terrific tale. "Having an agent" isn't the secret to selling your fiction—it's the secret to having better contracts and better income after you've already proven you can sell. It starts with you.

4. Classes and Workshops

Writing is lonely. It starts lonely and it only gets lonelier. And at the beginning you don't know if you're any good. You need an audience. You need advice from somebody who knows what he's doing. Heck, you need somebody to look at your work, nod his head, and say, "Yup, you're a writer."

So you look in your local college catalog and find a writing course. Or you get together with a bunch of friends who are also closet writers and you start reading each other's work. Or you hear about some terrific writing workshop that offers professional writers and you apply. Or you take a mail-order writing course.

And, depending on what you need and who you are, any of these could be wonderful — or a disaster.

Writing Workshops

You and a bunch of friends get together once a month to read each other's stories. You run up a huge photocopying bill, and when you're through with each session, you can't help wondering whether it's doing any good. After all, the other participants aren't published yet, either. Maybe they trash every story you bring — but does that mean your stories are no good or that they don't know how to recognize a good story when they see it?

Every workshop, whether it's composed of rank amateurs or experienced professionals, will give you three valuable things:

Company. Sometimes what you need most is to hear other people talking about writing with the same passion and anguish that you feel. After co-workers and family members have teased you for months about how you waste so much time writing made-up stories, meeting with fellow writers can be a great relief.

Deadlines. If you're writing part-time, it's often hard to get the sense of urgency necessary to make yourself sit down and *write*. And even when you do, you may keep fiddling with a story forever, never considering it to be finished. Knowing that you have to turn in something on Thursday helps you to get some kind of ending on the story, run off a bunch of copies, and put it into somebody else's hands.

Audience. Just having another human being read your story and respond to it can be gratifying. From a rejection slip you don't know whether a living human being ever looked at your tale. But in a workshop, you *know* they read it. You had a respectful audience that actually tried to pay attention to what you wrote.

Writing Classes

Writing classes at every level are usually taught by people who don't really know how to write. Precious few of them are taught by people who know how to *teach* writing.

Writing is very hard to teach, but it becomes almost impossible when the teacher, schooled in American college literature courses, believes that the critical approach he learned there has something to do with how his students should *write*.

That makes as much sense as trying to learn how to make wine by listening to a second-hand account of a wine critic.

"Nice bouquet," says the critic of a good wine.

The wine-making teacher listens, and then tells his students, "You've got to make sure your wine has a nice bouquet."

"How?" asks the student.

"I'm not sure, but this wine of yours certainly doesn't have it."

"Does the bouquet have something to do with using the right grapes?"

"I don't know about grapes," says the wine-making teacher disdainfully. "That's for *grape-growers*. I teach *wine*."

That's the problem with writing teachers trained solely in literature courses—they've studied only finished products that have already been judged to be "great." They've been taught to read them by decoding symbology and analyzing style. But great stories are not made by stringing together a bunch of symbols and deliberately creating a style.

The winemaker harvests the best grapes he can, crushes them, purifies the juice, and ages it in the way that seems right to him—and then trusts in natural processes to ferment the wine and transform the flavor. Likewise, the writer harvests the best and truest ideas he can, fits them together into a structure that makes sense to him, writes it with clarity, and trusts in his own natural voice and story-sense to bring forth all those marvelous things that critics look for. *True* symbols are as much a surprise to the author as to the reader; *true* style comes from the natural voice of the author, recorded in print. If you don't write symbols and style, they happen anyway. But well-created worlds, effective structures, and clarity don't just happen—they must be created consciously, and they *can* be learned.

There *are* writing teachers who actually know something that is useful to new writers—there are moments when I think I'm one of them. Even so, none of us can teach a student writer anything that he or she isn't *ready* to learn; and there isn't a thing we teach that a writer can't learn for himself.

So I think you *should* take classes from time to time. You just shouldn't expect that class to "teach you how to write."

If you have appropriate expectations, you won't be disappointed. Most

117

writing classes are conducted like workshops; if so, they'll deliver at least the minimum that every workshop delivers. And if by some great fluke you end up with a teacher who actually knows how to teach writing, be glad and learn all you can.

But if you intend to write speculative fiction, talk to the teacher *before* you ever sign up for the class. Tell him frankly that you intend to write science fiction or fantasy and ask him if that's acceptable. If the teacher reacts with amusement or scorn ("I teach students who aspire to create *literature*"), the class will almost certainly be a painful or frustrating experience. If the teacher has no objection, but warns you that he really doesn't know anything about speculative fiction, you might still take the class — but remember that half the time he probably won't even understand what you're trying to do. However, if the teacher reacts with some enthusiasm, go for it. Even if he doesn't know that much about sf, at least your stories will have a sympathetic audience.

If there is no class or workshop in your neighborhood — or none that will treat speculative fiction with respect — you might want to try joining — or starting — a class or workshop by mail. For several years, Kathleen Woodbury of Salt Lake City has run an excellent co-op writing workshop by mail, in which manuscripts are evaluated by several professional writers. Writer's Digest School is offering a speculative fiction writing course you can take by correspondence. If you have a computer with a modem, you can certainly find writing workshops conducted on-line. And there are doubtless other long-distance classes and workshops available if you look for them.

The Dangers of Workshops and Classes
Here's a short list of things that can go wrong and what to do about them.

We're a family. You hang out with the same people so long that you become dear friends. You *love* these guys. The trouble is, the better you like each other, the more sympathetic you become to each other's stories. You like Writer X so well you like her stories even when they're lousy. You're so familiar with Writer Y's quirks that you hardly notice anymore that his stories are almost unintelligible. You may have the greatest friendships of your life — but you don't have a workshop anymore.

Solution: Keep going to the parties, but find a new workshop for your stories.

Rapiers and scalpels. One or more workshop members specialize in being clever and witty at other writers' expense. They make personal attacks on the writer ("Only a fascist pig could write a character like this") or ridicule the story ("Even a paper shredder would be ashamed to swallow this") without saying anything that their victim can actually learn from.

Solution: Put a stop to ridicule or personal abuse. If they won't stop, kick out the offenders. And if the group won't kick them out, quit. This kind of viciousness is the enemy of art.

Is it Thursday again? In a burst of enthusiasm, the group agrees to meet weekly. You find that reading other writers' stories and attending the workshop uses up most of your writing time.

Solution: Cut back the schedule. If the group won't change, you start showing up less often. Or quit.

Lope de Vega syndrome. Lope de Vega was a great Spanish playwright who wrote something like a thousand plays in his lifetime. One wonders when he ate or slept. Sometimes one writer in a workshop produces so much that you end up reading his work every week, and yet he never seems to get any better. He's taking all the fun out of the workshop.

Solution: Limit each writer to no more than one submission a month (for instance). Or ask Lope de Vega to leave the group. Or quit.

I liked the old version better. You brought your first draft of the story to the workshop or class, and they gave you many helpful suggestions. You rewrote it and brought it back, and they still don't like it; or they like it fine, but it's still getting rejected by editors.

Solution: Never bring the same story back to the same workshop. They can't give it an honest reading a second time. If you made the changes they suggested, how can they now find fault with it? And if you didn't make those changes, how can you expect them to like it any better this time? By and large, a workshop will only help a story the first time it's read.

You're mismatched with the group. You find that nobody in the group is terribly interested in your stories; people tend to be kind to you, but it seems that their stories all work much better than yours and you can't figure out why. Or your stories are always so much better than anybody else's that they never have anything helpful to say, while they hang on every word you say about *their* stories as if you were the teacher.

Solution: Quit. You don't belong in this group.

Conferences

Where classes and workshops usually meet on a weekly or monthly schedule over a long period of time, conferences meet all day for only a few days or weeks in a row—and then they're done. You often pay a lot for a conference, including travel costs and the amount of time away from your job or your family. And you don't know until you have committed all that time and money whether it'll be any good or not. Is it worth going?

Conferences range from a series of lectures and readings by professionals, in which *your* stories are never read, to an extremely intense workshop in which you're expected to write and critique new stories throughout the conference. Some lecture conferences do give you a chance (usually for an additional fee) to have one of the professional writers or editors read your manuscript and consult with you about it. Some workshop conferences also offer readings and lectures. Before you give any conference a dime, find out exactly what it offers.

Lecture conferences. To be blunt, I think lecture conferences are valuable only for the friendships you make with fellow novices. Maybe one of the lecturers will tell you something valuable; maybe not. But they certainly can't tell you which ideas they teach apply directly to your own manuscript. And even if you pay for a private consultation, you're getting only the least dependable aspect of a writing class—the comments of the teacher. Just because you loved Writer X's latest novel doesn't mean that he'll have any notion what you should do to improve your story.

Clarion and Clarion West. Workshop conferences, however, can be powerful—or devastating. Within the field of speculative fiction, there are two workshops that, to certain writers, are well worth their tremendous cost in time and money. Each summer, about twenty writers who have passed the screening process and forked over a tidy sum—which barely covers costs—arrive in West Lansing, Michigan, for Clarion, while another twenty or so arrive in Seattle for Clarion West. (Despite the similarity in name, the two workshops are completely separate and must be applied for separately; but since Clarion West is modeled on Clarion, most of what I say about either applies to both.)

For six weeks these writers live together, read each other's stories, and write their brains out. The experience is intense, and many participants undergo major personality changes — usually temporary. Most years one or two burn out completely; they never write again. And those few who come to Clarion expecting to receive validation ("Yes, Agnes, you really *are* a fine writer!") are usually disappointed.

Coming to Clarion often means quitting your job or giving up your apartment or leaving your children with a grandparent. But if you're serious about learning to write better, it can be worth the sacrifice. First, you work with six different professional writers — one per week — who read and comment on your stories. Second, you get to know twenty other participants, and the friendships formed there can last for years, often graduating into long-term professional relationships. Third, you write at least six stories, usually more, in a white-hot creative climate. I've taught once at Clarion, twice at Clarion West, and I've seen many students learn more in a week than they have in years before.

But Clarion isn't for fragile people. It's a tough experience, and those who gain the most from it are often those who are already at the cusp of professionalism. If you're just starting out and completely uncertain of your identity as a writer, Clarion can be the end, not the beginning. But if you *know* you're a writer and want to put yourself through six weeks in a wringer to squeeze out every drop of talent hiding somewhere inside you, apply to Clarion.

Creating a Wise Reader

Rare is the writer who actually knows what he's written when it first comes out on paper. A passage you think is clear won't be. A character you think is fascinating will bore other people silly because you haven't yet grasped what it is that makes him interesting. But you won't know it — until someone else has read it and told you.

Who? Your workshop? A teacher?

They really can't do the job you need. You need someone to read it *now*, today, the minute you finish it. Someone who is committed to your career and wants you to succeed almost as much as you do.

In other words, you need a spouse or *very* close friend who is a brilliant critic.

Right, you say. My husband reads my stories, but all he ever says is, "Pretty good." If you press him, he says, "I *liked* it." Some brilliant critic.

Here's the good news: You can turn almost any intelligent, committed person into the Wise Reader you need. But first you have to understand that a Wise Reader is not someone to tell you what to do next — it's *someone to tell you what you have just done.* In other words, you want your spouse or friend to report to you, in detail and accurately, on the experience of reading your story.

The audience never lies. When I was a playwright, I learned something about audiences. *After* the performance, everybody lies and tells you it was wonderful. But during the performance of a play, the audience will never lie. By the way they lean forward in their seats, eyes riveted on the stage, they tell you that they're interested, tense, anxious — exactly what you want. Then, suddenly, a large number of them shift in their seats, glance down at their program — without meaning to, they're telling you that something's wrong with the play, you've lost their attention.

As a fiction writer, you can't watch what they do while they're reading your manuscript. But you can train one reader to notice his own process of reading and take notes that will help you find the weak spots in your manuscript. You want him to keep a record of symptoms — what the story *does* to him.

For this job, it's better if your Wise Reader is *not* trained in literature — he'll be less likely to try to give you diagnoses ("The characterization was thin") or, heaven help us, prescriptions ("You need to cut out all this description"). The Wise Reader doesn't imagine for a moment that he can tell you how to fix your story. All he can tell you is what it feels like to read it.

Questions. How do you train him? You ask questions:

Were you ever bored? Did you find your mind wandering? Can you tell me where in the story this was happening? (Let him take his time, look back through the story, find a place where he remembers losing interest.)

What did you think about the character named Magwall? Did you like him? Hate him? Keep forgetting who he was? (If he hates your character for the right reasons, that's good news; if he couldn't remember who he was from one chapter to the next, that's very *bad* news.)

Was there anything you didn't understand? Is there any section you had to read twice? Is there any place where you got confused? (The answers to such questions will tell you where exposition isn't handled well, or where the action is confusing.)

Was there anything you didn't believe? Any time when you said, "Oh, come on!" (This will help you catch clichés or places where you need to go into more detail in your world creation.)

What do you think will happen next? What are you still wondering about? (If what he read is a fragment, the answers to such questions will tell you what lines of tension you have succeeded in establishing; if what he read is the whole story, the answers to these questions will tell you what lines of tension you haven't resolved.)

You won't be asking such questions for long. Pretty soon your Wise Reader will learn to notice his own internal processes as he reads. He'll note points of confusion, unbelievability, cliché, boredom; he'll think about how he feels about characters and tell you afterward.

Through exactly this process of asking questions, I turned my wife, Kristine, into my Wise Reader very early in our marriage. Because of her responses and concerns, my work is many times better than it would otherwise have been. Also, she's part of every page of every story I write— instead of my writing being a point of conflict in our marriage, as it is for many other writers, it's one of the places where we're most closely involved with each other.

Of course, I had to treat her observations with respect. Even when her responses hurt my feelings, I had to thank her. Most important, I had to do something to address the issues she raised; she had to see that her observations were leading to adjustments in the manuscript. She has never prescribed—never told me what I ought to do.

But the quid pro quo is that I have never left any of the symptoms untreated. I always do *something* to address every problem she reports in her reading process. At first this was sometimes hard, because I would think she was "wrong." I quickly learned, however, that she can't possibly be wrong—the Wise Reader never is. Why? Because the Wise Reader is reporting on his or her own experience of reading. How can she be *wrong* about her own experience?

Maybe sometimes Kristine's reaction to something in my story has been a private reaction—no one else would be bothered by the problem she uncovered. But I've always found—*always*—that once I started changing the problem aspect of the story, I improved it.

And now Kristine is so skilled at reading a story and so familiar with the things I do to fix certain problems, that she knows before I do exactly what changes I'll make. This can be disconcerting, like when a friend or spouse starts finishing your sentences for you, but it's also comforting to know how well she knows me.

She paid a terrible price for becoming my Wise Reader, however. Now she reads *everything* the way she reads my fiction, noticing when she's bored, when she doesn't believe, when she's confused, when she doesn't care about a character, when a plot question is unresolved. It spoils an awful lot of books and stories for her. But we think it's worth it. And when I turn in a fiction manuscript, we're both sure that it's ready to publish as it is.

5. Collaboration and Adaptation

At some point in your career, you'll decide to work with another writer or group of writers on a project.

Collaboration. When two write the same story together, it's called collaboration. It might seem that having two writers work on the same story would divide the work in half, but many collaborators report that it's more like twice the work. That's because in a true collaboration, both writers have to agree on everything. It can mean endless rewrites and painful compromises; it can mean having to put your name on a story that includes things that seem hopelessly wrong to you.

Yet it can also result in some of the best work of your career, if you and your collaborator can produce, together, something beyond the ability of either of you alone. After all, the great works of film and theatre, dance and music are usually collaborations of writer/director/choreographer/ composer and many performers who together create what no one of them could possibly produce alone. Is it surprising that sometimes collaboration in fiction can have good results?

Before you enter into a collaboration, however, make sure you have agreed on certain key points. Either of you should have the right to withdraw from the collaboration at any point — but then which of you will have the right to continue alone? Money is always split 50/50 except in the most extraordinary circumstances — but whose agent will handle the sale? Do both of you have to give consent for any publication of the work? In the rush of creativity, raising these questions might feel as awkward as handing your spouse-to-be a pre-nuptial agreement on the morning of the wedding—but it must be done, or there's a possibility of real rancor later.

Shared worlds. Shared-world anthologies comprise stories that take place in the same milieu. Each author is generally free to use characters from the other authors' stories, as long as the character's originator approves of what you have him do. The result can be quite exciting—different styles and visions combined into one interlaced network of tales. The world can seem quite real to the reader, in large part because of the fact that, as in the real world, each character is going his own way, touching the lives of others at times but not always caught up in their stories.

The most famous and successful shared world anthology series is *Thieves' World*, which essentially invented the formula that the others all follow—and, in the process, set up what seems to be a complicated but fair communitarian model of sharing the profits from joint creative endeavors. Other anthology series have had varying degrees of commercial success: *Liavek* was a career launcher for a group of Minnesota writers who got together in the best Andy Hardy fashion and decided to create their own books; established writers C. J. Cherryh, George R. R. Martin, and Andre Norton also started shared-world projects; and there have been many others begun and, occasionally, published.

Artistically, the technique is to begin with a simple situation that allows for endless complication. *Liavek* stories were centered around the single city of Liavek, which was thoroughly invented by a group of writers brainstorming together; they took great pains to make it a city with many different classes, guilds, religions, and other communities so that plenty of different characters could bump into each other in the course of a book. *Heroes in Hell* had an even simpler premise—all the dead are together in Hell, continuing to be who they were during mortality. This allowed writers to put together, say, Mark Twain and William Shakespeare, or Adolf Hitler and Albert Schweitzer, or whatever other combination of historical personages intrigued them. *Wild Cards* developed a premise for having a group of comic-book-style superheroes on the loose in a (relatively) plausible version of our beloved planet Earth. All these shared worlds did a good job of narrowly defining the range of the stories, so that each writer's work would be likely to intersect with the stories of other writers—and yet having enough variety *within* that narrow range that writers of very different tastes and interests could still tell tales within it.

Each shared world has its own financial arrangements, ranging from complete communalism—all participants receive shares of all volumes of the work from the time they joined the project—to the standard anthology arrangement in which each author is paid royalties only on the book in which his story appears, and only in proportion to the length of his story relative to all others.

How do you get involved in a shared world? You usually have to be invited to get into early volumes; later, some shared-world anthologies do open up to submissions from authors outside the original group. Some new authors who would never have been invited into someone else's shared world have developed their own shared-world anthologies together. But you should be aware that the market for shared worlds is pretty much glutted, now that the novelty has worn off. Still, there's room for a few new ones now and then on publishers' lists, and the success of *Thieves' World*, *Wild Cards*, *Liavek*, *Heroes in Hell*, and others almost guarantees that shared worlds will be around for many years to come.

Adaptations. "You've seen the movie; now read the book!" The movie came from an original screenplay, but several weeks before the movie comes out, there's a book on the stands. Novelizations, they're called—and the books based on *E.T.*, *Batman*, and many other films have reached the bestseller lists.

The authors of these books are usually paid a bit more up front than the average first novel advance—but their percentage of royalties is far lower, so that a monster hit won't mean that much more money to the novelizer than a complete failure. Also, writing a novelization can be a frustrating experience, since you almost always have to work from the screenplay, turning in your manuscript before filming has been completed. Often the whole plot of the movie will be changed in filming or editing, and there sits your book, with the old "wrong" version firmly enshrined.

Novelizations *can* be fine pieces of work, but in most cases very few readers and *no* critics will notice or care. There's little joy in the work, it does nothing for your career, and whether the money is worth it to you is for you to answer. Some novelists whose agents get them a shot at novelizations regard them as a chance to learn their craft using someone else's story—and that can be a good learning experience. But it *is* someone else's story, and you have almost no chance of influencing it significantly. I've done one novelization under highly unusual circumstances (I worked from finished film, not the screenplay; the director was committed to having an excellent novel; and the money was orders of magnitude better than normal) and I'm proud of the result. But I guarantee that you won't match those circumstances very often, and even if you do, you'll probably find as I did that you regret the books of your own that did not get written while you were working on the novelization.

6. Finances

Speculative fiction can pay decently now — but it's only in recent years that more than a handful of sf writers have been able to live solely from their writing. For every writer who hits fast and hard there are a dozen whose careers build slowly — and far more whose careers consist of a few stories and novels spread out over many years, with never enough income to live on.

Don't quit your job. In other words, when you get that contract for a first novel, don't quit your job. Five thousand bucks can seem like a lot of money until you realize that to reach the national median income ($25,000 at the time of this writing) you have to write five books a year at that price.

Only you can't be sure that you can actually produce five publishable books a year. And if you do, you run the risk of being perceived as a hack who turns out lots of books of middling quality. It's rare for writers of that reputation to get advances large enough to free them to write one or two really *fine* books a year.

Even when you do earn enough money to live on, it comes erratically and undependably. Royalty checks are often late (though when you ask them, most publishers will forget that they have ever been a bit tardy with payments) and there are many ugly surprises ("I'm sorry, but we had to raise your reserve against returns, so there's no money for you this time"). That's assuming that your books ever earn out their advance and start paying royalties — it wasn't until my ninth sf book that I ever received royalties beyond the original advance, and I was generally perceived as having a pretty strong career from the start.

In America we live in a world financially organized around the lunar cycle; writers don't fit too well in that world. Making monthly payments means saving money so that you can keep paying rent and bills during the six months between checks. That's fine if you happen to have the money to save; it breaks down a bit when it happens to be eight months between checks this time instead of the normal six. In other words, if writing is your sole source of income, your credit rating can go down the toilet in a few months while your publishers work out their "cash flow" problems (meaning that they only have enough money to pay their printer, and too bad about you).

You may dream of getting free of your daily job so instead of writing your stories in stolen moments—at night, at lunch, on weekends—you can devote full time to your art. But how easy is it to produce deathless prose when you're worried sick about money? When every phone call might be a creditor?

If I paint a dark picture of the financial side of a writer's life, it's because the picture is often *very* dark. Unless you are independently wealthy or have a spouse who's willing to support your writing habit or relatives who can bail you out in troublous times, think very carefully before you quit your steady, secure job.

Besides, that job keeps you out in the world, in contact with other people—with potential stories and characters. Many who quit their jobs discover the hard way that they produce no more fiction than they did when they were writing only in stolen moments.

Handling the money. If you examine your expenses and your writing income and determine that you *can* make it, then do it right. Nobody withholds taxes for you. The money passes through your hands; therefore it becomes tempting to spend it and take your taxes out of "the next check." I speak from experience: This leads to disaster. Estimate your state and federal income tax on every single check you receive; put that tax in the bank immediately and never, never spend it except to file your quarterly estimated tax returns. There is no grief from agents or publishers or even critics that can compare with the grief that comes when you get behind on your taxes.

In addition to your tax account, maintain a cash reserve, and build it up to the point where you have a year's income in the bank. Trust me: you'll need it. The big payday that comes today doesn't guarantee you'll have anything like that next year. Back in 1980 I was flying high—I'd signed one contract for $75,000 and another for $30,000. I thought it would go on like that, a steady upward curve. Instead, during the recession of the early eighties the publishers panicked, and I found myself listening to offers of $7500 — or outright refusals to buy. I knew that accepting an advance like that would be a deadly step backward; I had to go back to work for about a year in order to keep my advance levels where they needed to be.

Writing is no different from movies or sports or any of the other high-risk professions. For a few, there's wealth and fame; for most of us, there are shocking ups and downs. When you have an up, save for the next down. When you have a $50,000 year after five years at $15,000, don't start living as though you were pulling down $50,000 every year — because next year you might make nothing at all.

Speculative fiction is wide open, and you *can* make a living at it with the right combination of talent, luck, drive — and financial self-discipline. Unfortunately, the very attributes that make you a wonderful storyteller may work against your being very good at managing money. If that's the case with you, as it is with me, be honest enough to admit it to yourself and turn your money management over to somebody else. In my case, I had the good sense to marry a grown-up. Kristine handles the money; I don't even carry a checkbook. Life works better for us that way. You figure out what will work well for you, and then stick with it.

7. Joining the Club

Speculative fiction is a lively literary community, with strong participation from readers, writers, editors, and critics. You may already be aware of "fandom" — the conventions every weekend, the fanzines, the clubs. Or you may follow the professional and critical community — the professional organizations, the awards, the review columns, the critical journals. Or you may have caught only a glimpse of all that activity — the Hugo and Nebula awards, the best-of-the-year anthologies, the quotes from other authors on the covers of new books.

The fact is that even before you become a published author of speculative fiction you can be actively involved at almost every level of this community of people drawn together by wonderful stories in strange worlds.

Conventions
Most major cities in America have at least one convention a year. Some conventions have different emphases: Some focus on film and television

sf, some are primarily for people who like to dress up in elaborate costumes from fiction and film, some are for people who like to play sf games, and some are for serious critical and literary discussion. Most, though, include a little bit of everything. There are almost always a couple of famous guests and quite a few not-so-famous ones.

The biggest convention is the World Science Fiction Convention, whose location changes from year to year (in recent years: Los Angeles; Atlanta; Brighton, England; New Orleans; Boston). Put on entirely by amateurs, WorldCon is a remarkable event and practically everybody is there. For a nearly complete listing of upcoming conventions, check *Locus* or most issues of *Isaac Asimov's Science Fiction Magazine*. You'll probably find a convention near you.

Once you've started selling stories, if you let your local convention know about it, they will gladly put you on some panels and give you a chance to talk about the things you care about. Let me give you a few hints about how to do this successfully:

Be modest. Even though they're dressed up in costumes and often include people who don't dress for success, the audiences at sf convention panels and events are generally a good deal brighter than the population at large, and they can smell a phony from fifty yards away. They are not googly-eyed at the sight of a Real Writer like you — most of them have had discussions with Harlan Ellison or Isaac Asimov or Carolyn Cherryh or Larry Niven at conventions like these, and they're not going to treat you with much deference or respect.

So don't spend all your time talking about your latest book — they probably don't care, and if you push yourself too strongly, there's almost certainly someone in the audience who *did* read your book and didn't like it and won't be shy about telling you and the rest of the audience why. But if you talk about ideas and do so with intelligence and passion — even if you aren't a terrific public speaker — the audience will warm to you and help you. *Real* people are well treated by fandom; phonies get chewed up and spat out.

Don't let it take over your life. There is a convention every weekend of the year somewhere in the U.S. As your work begins to catch on, people will take more notice of you. You'll get invited to a lot of these conventions. Some may even offer to help pay your way or give you a free room; most will give a free membership to professional writers (i.e., people who've published something). If you're a frustrated actor like me, you'll thrive on the chance to perform; if you're just plain lonely, you'll grasp at the chance to be with people who care about fiction.

Furthermore, at the bigger conventions you meet a lot of writers and editors. You talk shop. You get taken to dinner in fancy places. It's easy to convince yourself that you *have* to go to Convention X—it's part of the business. And it *is* part of the business, now and then.

It's possible, though, to get too caught up in the convention life. It's professionally good to be visible; it's personally and artistically debilitating to be ubiquitous. Some writers seem to live in the bar at conventions—one wonders when they're sober enough to touch type. Other writers simply stop writing for long stretches—their time is all taken up with fandom. If you find that conventions and fandom interfere with your writing, make sure that the writing takes precedence. The conventions will go just fine without you for a while.

Professional Organizations

The Science Fiction Writers of America has a misleading name—many of the members are from the United Kingdom and Canada, with a few from places like the Soviet Union, Japan, Germany, and France; many of the members write fantasy, never science fiction; and there are some members who have never written a story in their lives. Be that as it may, the SFWA is one of the most powerful—and quarrelsome—professional organizations in the arts.

SFWA is *not* a union—you won't ever be asked to go on strike. It isn't cheap, either—the dues are stiff. But SFWA has, over the years, under strong leadership and through great solidarity, managed to perform some miracles. They have audited the books of publishers accused of dishonesty or carelessness, and arranged payments to members; they have convinced several publishers to withdraw or revise obnoxious contracts; and, through their hardworking grievance committees, they have done much to help individual members in their struggles with publishers, editors, and agents.

Also, the SFWA nominates and votes on the annual Nebula Awards, the "academy awards" of science fiction. Whether you think the award actually goes to the "best" work of the year is relatively unimportant—what matters is that the members care deeply and passionately about what constitutes good science fiction and fantasy, and those concerns are brought to the fore during the annual nominating and voting. And when the results are announced and published, the message to the reading public is clear: The writers of speculative fiction are concerned about recognizing excellence in their field; this is an art, not just a business.

It's good to remember these accomplishments when you see all the bickering and sniping at SFWA meetings and in the pages of SFWA's free-for-all magazine, the *Forum*. Part of being a literary community means that there's some friction, and since we're all skilled rhetoricians, the language can sometimes be quite colorful. Most SFWA members, however, are kindly, well-mannered souls who shudder at the behavior of a few compatriots. And even the "livelier" types can turn out to be your friends or mentors in times of need. If the level of friction — and heat — troubles you, look into the history of any young literature and you'll find the same sort of thing. To date SFWA seems to have had far fewer cases of bodily assault than, say, the eighteenth-century English literary crowd, so perhaps we're not so bad.

The membership requirements are simple: a few publications in professional magazines or a single published novel will bring you full membership; for associate membership, dues are lower and requirements are even easier. The current address of SFWA's executive secretary, Peter Pautz, is:

SFWA
Peter D. Pautz, Exec. Sec.
Box H
Wharton NJ 07885

Pautz deals with all questions concerning membership eligibility.

There are other writers' organizations, most notably the new Horror Writers Association, modeled closely on the best features of SFWA. Check with *Locus* or your publisher or editor if you're a professional writer interested in getting information about pertinent professional organizations.

8. Awards

Besides the Nebula Award, the other major sf award is the Hugo, given out at the annual WorldCon. Voted on by members of the convention (you must join many months in advance if you want to nominate and vote for the Hugos), the Hugos are given in many more categories than the Nebulas. Fiction Nebulas and Hugos are given in the standard four categories: Short story (1-7,499 words), Novelette (7,500-14,999), Novella (15,000-39,999), and Novel (40,000 words and longer). Hugos are also awarded in other categories, like best nonfiction, best artist, best professional editor, and in fan categories like best fanzine, best fan writer, and best fan artist. WorldCon also votes on the John W. Campbell Award for Best New Writer, for which a writer is eligible for two years following his first publication.

There are many other awards of great distinction: The Campbell Memorial Award for novel (voted on by a jury), the Sturgeon Memorial Award for short fiction (jury), the Philip K. Dick Award for original paperback novel (jury), the World Fantasy Awards in several categories (jury, with some nominations by members of the World Fantasy Convention); many awards in foreign countries, including the "Japanese Hugos" customarily presented at WorldCon; and many awards by less-well-known organizations. It can be a heady thing to win any of these awards, and in all cases the awards are a symbol of a devotion to quality. The speculative fiction community cares very much about literary quality, even if we define it in our own terms.

A word of advice, however: Writers do not campaign for awards unless they are prepared to reap a harvest of scorn. The slightest hint of anything even resembling campaigning leads to a great deal of nastiness and suspicion, so even though most writers do harbor secret ambitions of receiving Hugos and Nebulas, it's considered more decorous to appear unconcerned when one's own story goes before the voters.

There is also a great deal of talk about how the major awards — Hugos and Nebulas — lead to wealth and fame. It's true that foreign sales generally rise for authors who have won these awards (foreign editors often have few other guides as to who is "hot" in the U.S., which remains the heart of science fiction), but many winners will tell you that a Hugo or Nebula is no guarantee that a work will even remain in print.

In short, while it's lovely to receive awards, they should be appreciated for what they mean: that a certain number of people like your work. Don't expect any more than that, and certainly don't make the slightest change in your writing or your behavior in an attempt to win one. If you win, fine; if you don't, that's also fine. The awards rarely go to the most innovative writers until long after their best work is done.

9. Life at Home

I don't know you; it would be presumptuous of me to try to tell you how to live. Nevertheless, I've seen enough other writers and had enough experiences of my own to be able to warn you of some dangers and point out some things that may work for you. If you don't like people preaching at you, skip this section, because that's pretty much what I'm about to do. But if you are willing to listen to the observations of somebody who has lived this life for more than a few years, and has watched many other writers from varying degrees of distance, then this section is for you: The advice here has as much to do with becoming and remaining a successful writer as any other part of this book.

Discipline. The life of a full-time writer has no externally imposed discipline. No one expects you in the morning; if you're late to work, no one glowers. You can take a day off whenever you want, and you never need a note from a doctor. No one hires a temp to take your place if you're gone for a week. This means you are deliciously free; it also means that if, like me, you are extravagantly lazy, you can find yourself way behind in your work.

The discipline has to come from within. Don't wait for a muse to strike and force you to your typewriter. Such events are rare—in my experience, muses tend to strike those who are at the keyboard typing their brains out, not those who are playing video games in the basement.

Take care of your body. Writing is a sedentary business; it's easy for many of us to get fat and sluggish. Your brain is attached to the rest of your body. You can't do your best work when you're weak or in ill health. At times when I've exercised and kept my weight down, I've had much more vigor and stamina when it came to writing. At other times, when I've neglected my health, I've struggled to pull energetic stories out of a lethargic mind. It's worth the time to take an hour's walk before writing. You may write a bit less for the time spent, but you may find that you write better.

Beware of dependencies. Writing is self-exhaustive. Everything you produce comes out of your own soul. You don't always like what you find there, and you always fear that someday you'll reach down inside yourself for something and find nothing there at all. There's a lot of tension in that, and no easy way to dissipate it. It's quite easy to become dependent on the reassurance that comes from drugs: caffeine, alcohol, and sometimes harder stuff.

When you become dependent on such things, they fulfill the fear they're often intended to quell: They make it harder to tell stories, harder to find truthful things to say, and harder to communicate them clearly. There are those who claim they can't write without their coffee or booze or some pharmaceutical crutch. I believe that the truth is much more painful: They can't *live* without those things, so they certainly can't *write* without them, as long as the dependency remains.

How serious are you about your art? Your mind is your instrument. How can you tell the truth unless your vision's clear?

Be patient. What is it you want? To write? Or to be a writer? If you want to *be* a writer — to have the fame and fortune that you imagine writers have — you'll have a long wait. But if you want to do what writers do — tell stories that other people may or may not want to read — you'll enjoy your life whether your stories catch on with the public or not.

Don't try to find shortcuts. A lasting career only comes from learning the craft and working hard to perfect it. And even if a degree of fame or praise does come quickly and easily, don't count on it continuing. The critic who loved this year's book will rip you up and down next year; the public that bought a hundred thousand copies of the last book may buy only ten thousand of the next. Bear it calmly. Fame comes and goes, but you — your life, your work, your family, your real friends — will still be there, year in and year out.

Don't compete or compare. It's deadly to start comparing yourself to other writers. Why did *he* win the Nebula this year when *my* story is so much better? How did *she* get a six-figure contract when I published my first story five years before anybody ever heard of her? I must really be a failure, if I can't do better than *he* does.

I've been on both sides of that awful fence between the envied and the envious, and this much is clear: There is no rational basis for comparison or competition in the arts. If somebody gets rich and famous faster than you, it may mean they're better at the craft than you are — or it may mean they happen to be telling stories that strike a nerve with a wider audience. What happens to other writers says nothing about you or your talent or your future. The writer you envy today will probably have reason to envy you tomorrow.

And envy is poisonous. One person's success doesn't take anything

135

away from you. If two people write brilliant books that are published the same day, the shine from one doesn't diminish the lustre of the other. If the audience goes crazy about one book and buys a million copies in a month, that doesn't stop another book from selling a million copies the same month. In fact, the success of one sf book generally brings new readers into the field — some of whom will discover and love *your* works.

One of the nicest things about the field of speculative fiction is how *little* envy there is. Older writers almost always reach out to help younger ones; younger ones almost always give honor to the older ones. Even where there are squabbles, there's almost always an underlying respect that wins out in the long run. The enemy of a good writer is never another writer — the enemy is apathy and unconcern in the audience. That's what you need to overcome if you're going to succeed in your art, and in *that* struggle we writers are all on the same side.

Keep perspective. Storytelling *is* important. You really *do* have an effect on the world, and it matters that you write your tales and have them published. But other things matter, too — your family, your friends. I've known more than a few writers who forget how to be decent human beings, who act as though their status as writers lifted them above such common limitations as courtesy and generosity, patience and good humor.

It's especially important to remain on good terms with the people you live with. Writing puts many strains on family life. When you're just starting out, your spouse and children may think those evening and weekend hours you spend typing are stolen from them. Sometimes you *do* have to finish the story; sometimes, though, your family and friends need you more than art does.

And later, when your career is moving well, it's easy to be seduced by people who treat you as if everything you say is clever and fascinating. Your spouse and kids can never compete with the adulation of strangers; they know you too well. It's so easy to forget who you are and fall into the famous-writer role that strangers may want you to fill. It happens to those who are weak or unwary. It helps to take a few moments now and then and decide whether you would let any of your fictional heroes treat other people the way you do — or, if they did, whether you would like them very much. A bit of self-examination now and then is also good for your fiction, since all your characters come, ultimately, from inside you.

The best storytellers are the ones who write, not to get rich and famous, but because they love good stories and long to share them with other people. That's a fundamentally positive act. Even if your stories happen to be grimy or frightening or depressing, telling those stories is an act of union between two or more human beings. Even if you think you believe in nothing, you believe in *that*, or you wouldn't bother to tell your tales in the first place. Even the most "anti-social" fiction is, fundamentally, a community-building act.

The community built by speculative fiction is a particularly important one, because it includes, as audience and storytellers, many of the people who are most open to change and most accepting of strangeness. They are the visionaries, the cutting edge of society, the people who in their hearts are explorers and pioneers — and they draw some of their visions and receive some of their experiences from the work we offer them. It's a labor worth doing, and worth doing well.

So close this book and get back to work.

Index

evolution of aliens, 50-52
experimental stories, 11-12, 108
exposition, 88-100

Fantasy and Science Fiction, Magazine of, 6, 12, 14
Face in the Abyss (Merritt), 8
"Faithful Companion at 40" (Karen Joy Fowler), 11
fandom, 129-131
fantasy; boundaries of, 20-24; development of genre, 6; heroic, 108; marketing, 110; rustic, 7
fanzines, 107-108
finances of writer, 127-129
first draft, 33-34
foreign markets, 109-110, 133
formulas, 16, 58-59
Forum (SFWA), 132
Forward, Robert, 57-58, 59
Free Live Free (Wolfe), 12
"From Elfland to Poughkeepsie" (LeGuin), 100
fuel mass to fuel energy ratio, 38, 41

Geary, Patricia, 12
generation ships, 40-42
Gernsback, Hugo, 9
ghettoizing of speculative fiction, 9-11
Good-bye, Mr. Chips (Hilton), 9
Gulliver's Travels (Swift), 76

Haggard, H. Rider, 7, 8-9, 25
Hamlet, (Shakespeare), 81
hard science fiction, 58-61
Hart's Hope (Orson Scott Card), 32
Hayakawa's SF magazine, 109
Heechee novels (Pohl), 39
Heinlein, Robert, 6, 14, 39, 92
Helliconia trilogy (Aldiss), 60
Herbert, Frank, 6, 10, 16
hero, 66-67
Heroes in Hell, 125
Hersey, John, 10
Hilton, James, 9
history of created world, 52-53
Hobbit, The (Tolkien), 6
home life, 133-137
Horror Writers Association, 132
horror fiction, 18-19, 108; marketing, 110
Hugo Awards, 7, 12, 129, 132-133
Huxley, Aldous, 61
hyperspace, 38-40

idea stories, 77-78, 84-85
ideas, finding and developing, 33-36
Illiad (Homer), 18, 83
implication, 91-92

imprints, publisher's, 21
Indiana Jones movies, 79
Interzone, 109
Invisible Man (Wells), 8
Irving, John, 16

jargon, 56-57
Journey to the Center of the Earth (Verne), 8

King Must Die, The (Renault), 30
King, Stephen, 18-19
Knight, Damon, 12

language, 100-103; invented, 53-57
LeGuin, Ursula K., 10, 14, 44, 100
Liavek, 125
Lindholm, Megan, 14, 82
literalism, 92-94
Locus, 107, 130
Lord of the Rings (Tolkien), 6, 54, 82
Lost Horizon (Hilton), 9

MICE Quotient, 76-76, 83-86
Macbeth (Shakespeare), 82
magazines, 6-7, 105-106
magic, price of, 31-32; rules of, 23-24, 47-49
mail classes or workshops, 118
main character, 66-70
markets; for short fiction, 105-110; for novels, 110; for fantasy, 7, 110
Martin, George R.R., 125
McCaffrey, Anne, 6, 10, 14
Member of the Wedding (Carson McCullers), 79
Merritt, A., 7, 8-9, 25
metaphor, 92-93
Midsummer Night's Dream, A (Shakespeare), 102
milieu, 19, 57-62; story, 76-77, 83-86
Miss Manners, 100
Moondust and Madness (Jenelle Taylor), 18
Morrow, 110
movie rights, 114
multiple submission/query, 111-112
My Petition for More Space (Hersey), 10
mystery fiction, 72, 77-78
myth, 16; of the story, 73

NAL/Signet, 110
naming characters, 90-91
Nebula Awards, 7, 12, 129, 131-133
Neverness (David Zindell), 24
1984 (Orwell), 17
"Ninth Symphony of Ludwig von Beethoven and Other Lost Songs" (Carter Scholz), 46